THE ARTS
SOCIETY
BEDS & HERTS

CONTENTS

FIFTY
TREASURES
OF THE
BEDS & HERTS
AREA

Unless otherwise stated all photographs included in this book are attributed to Richard Burn LRPS and Neil Harris.

THE ARTS SOCIETY
BEDS & HERTS

INTRODUCTION & THANKS

This book is one of a series being produced by various areas of the UK on behalf of The Arts Society (previously known as NADFAS). Beds & Herts Area consists of 17 Societies, details of which can be found at the back of this book. Each Society holds monthly lectures on a huge variety of arts-related topics such as art history, paintings, sculpture, architecture, photography, music, gardens, museums, historic collections – I could go on and on. The lecturers have passed very stringent tests before being approved, so the standard is exceptionally high. In addition to lectures, Societies arrange Special Interest Days where topics are looked at in more detail, as well as visits to nearby places of interest and trips away.

If you are not already a member, I urge you to look at what your nearest Society can offer – what better way to spend an hour or so learning something new amongst like-minded people, with a chance to chat over a cup of coffee or even a glass of wine!

The ideas for our 50 Treasures have come from our members, for which I am very grateful – some I know and some I am really looking forward to visiting. The book has been brought about by the hard work and dedication of a sub-group consisting of

Ian Burgess (Chair), Caroline Barnes (Editor), Colin Robinson, Anne Harris, Karen Brady, Richard Burn and myself. Unless otherwise stated, the splendid photographs have been taken by Richard Burn LRPS and Neil Harris.

The book would not have been produced without the help and support of the Societies within our Area and I thank them for backing this project, even in the unprecedented times of the Covid pandemic. Profits from sales of this book will be used to aid community art projects in the Area such as funding specialist equipment for schools, art therapists in children's hospital wards and hospices, art competitions in prisons and awarding grants to art students and museums.

I hope that it will adorn your coffee tables as well as be a regular item in your cars and rucksacks as you explore and learn about the history and heritage of our fascinating area – full of wonderful historic and religious buildings, fascinating museums, well-known and lesser-known objets d'art, gardens and much more. Have fun!

GILL BURN
Chair

The Arts Society Beds & Herts Area Team

THE ARTS SOCIETY

FOREWORD
FROM JULIE GOLDSMITH
CHAIR OF THE ARTS SOCIETY

The brutalist M1 motorway cuts a swathe through Beds & Herts. Take time to branch off and within minutes be enjoying its charming towns, villages and associated cultural offerings. Magnificent churches, gardens, houses and museums and a plethora of hidden treasures tucked away, tantalisingly close to our capital city.

Members of The Arts Society, locals of these two counties, have carefully curated a selection of their favourites. Their collection of *Fifty Treasures* will be invaluable as a reminder of what is on the doorstep and perhaps inspire others to explore further afield knowing these particular choices have a local seal of approval.

Having spent most of my early life in this part of the world, it is an honour to be asked to write this foreword to the latest in our hugely popular series of *50 Treasures*. Many of the places are already known to me but many aren't. It is this mix of the expected and unexpected that makes this series of books so compelling. Congratulations and thanks to members on the publication of the latest edition. Enjoy!

Congregational Chapel
Roxton

Following Congregational tradition this building is referred to as 'the Chapel' and members of its congregation as 'the Church'. This delightful Grade II listed chapel began as a lowly barn belonging to Charles Metcalfe of Roxton Park. He donated the barn to be licensed "for occasional worship by ministers of different denominations" and services commenced in May 1808.

The Nonconformist Church obtained a full licence in 1823 and appointed the first minister. The building remained unaltered until approximately 1833 when wings were added to accommodate children.

Rural life for 'the Church' continued remarkably undisturbed. For example, in December 1944, despite the explosion of a German V1 in a nearby field plunging the Chapel into darkness, worship was concluded with the Benediction. Services continue to be held in this hidden gem.

Further Information

1

High Street, Roxton, MK44 3EB.

www.roxtonchapel.btck.co.uk

Access: Open for services and tours. Please check website for details.

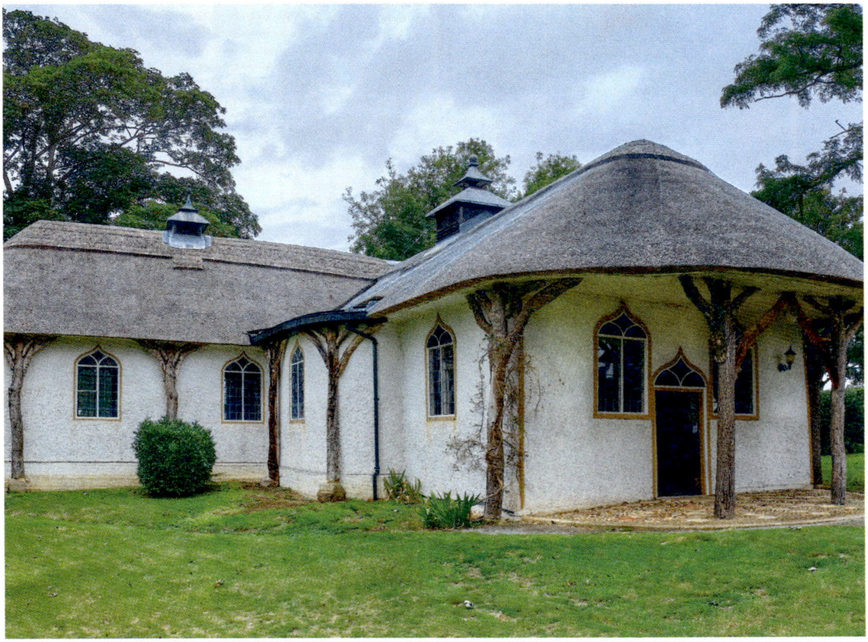

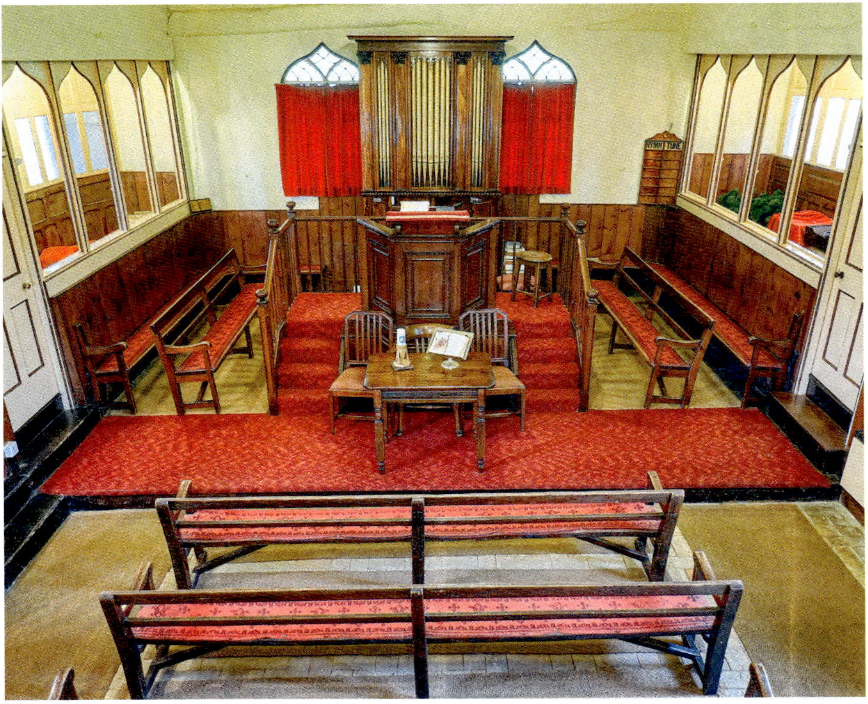

Kathy Brown's Garden
Stevington

Situated in the picturesque village of Stevington, north of Bedford, the garden is laid out in various sections. Many of these 'art gardens' are inspired by the work of famous artists such as Matisse, Monet, Hokusai, Barbara Hepworth and Barnett Newman.

It is a delight to stroll through whilst admiring numerous floral displays, the wisteria walk, ornamental grasses, the apple and pear orchard and garden ornaments. Lovingly created over the last 25 years by the current owners, the 4.5 acre garden and the Manor House have historic ties dating back many centuries. It is believed that there has been a garden on this site since the 13th century when it was associated with a holy well and the healing of eyes.

Further Information

2

The Manor House, Church Road, Stevington, Nr Bedford, MK43 7QB.

www.kathybrownsgarden.com

Access: Part of National Garden Scheme. The gardens are mostly accessible by wheelchair.

What's Nearby: Stevington Windmill
www.bedford.gov.uk/leisure-and-culture/arts-and-culture/history-and-heritage/stevington-mill

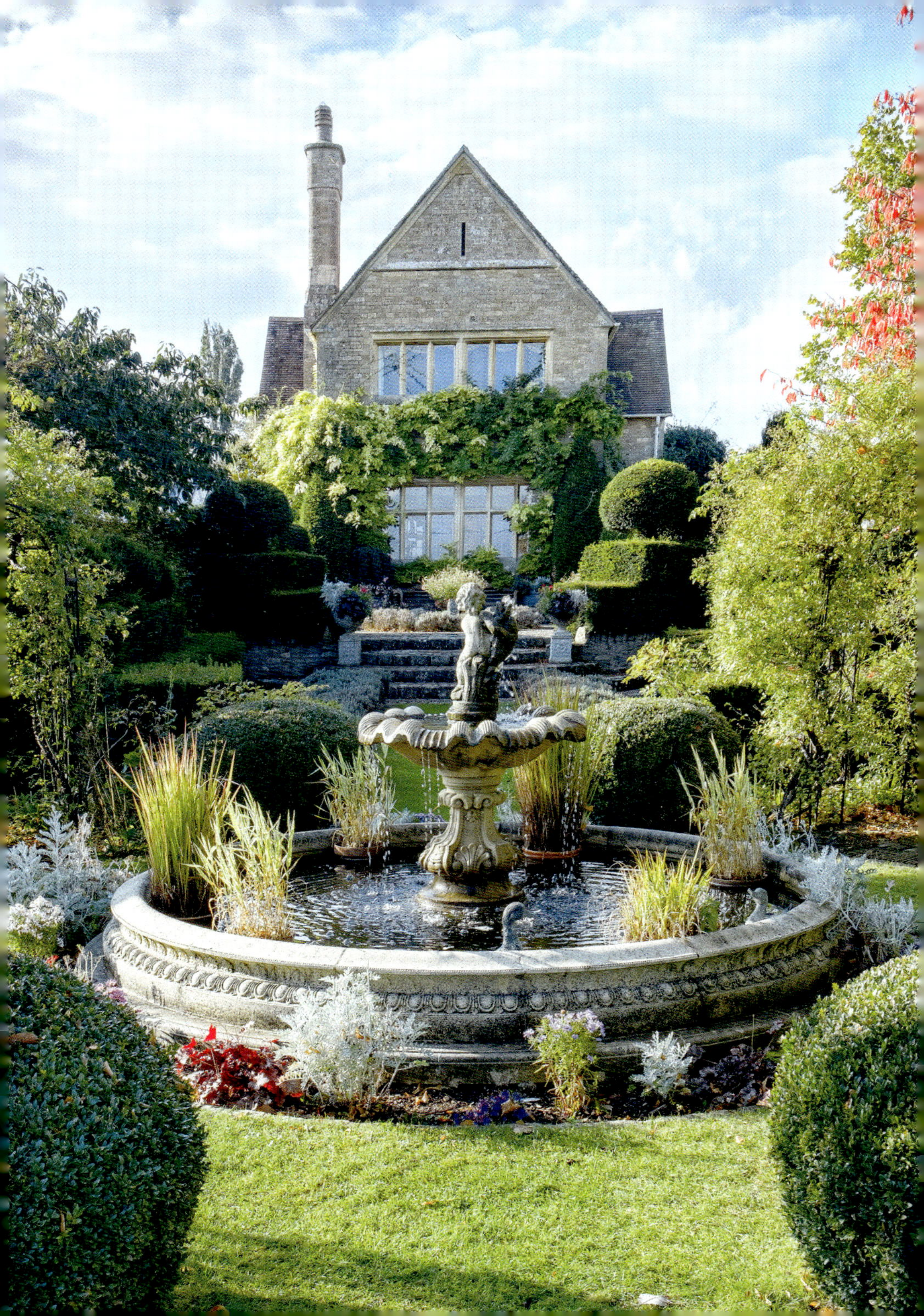

Foster Hill Road Cemetery
Bedford

Bedford's first municipal cemetery opened in 1855 and covers approximately 37 acres. A wealth of historical interest can be found amongst the 50,000 memorials, representing 100,000 burials. It offers examples of virtually every popular design of Victorian headstone. The Gothic revival style chapel was originally separated into two, one for Church of England and one for Dissenters. With no further room for burials, the cemetery, which is also an arboretum with rare and interesting trees, is part of Bedford's heritage of historical monuments and a quiet recreational area. A grid location map can assist identifying specific graves.

One section is a designated County Wildlife Site and contains rare plant species including several types of orchid. A variety of birds, butterflies and other creatures can be observed throughout the year, specifically woodpeckers, birds of prey and bats.

Further Information

3

Foster Hill Road, Bedford, MK41 7TD.

www.fosterhillroadcemetery.co.uk

Access: Unlimited pedestrian access daily - please check website for times.

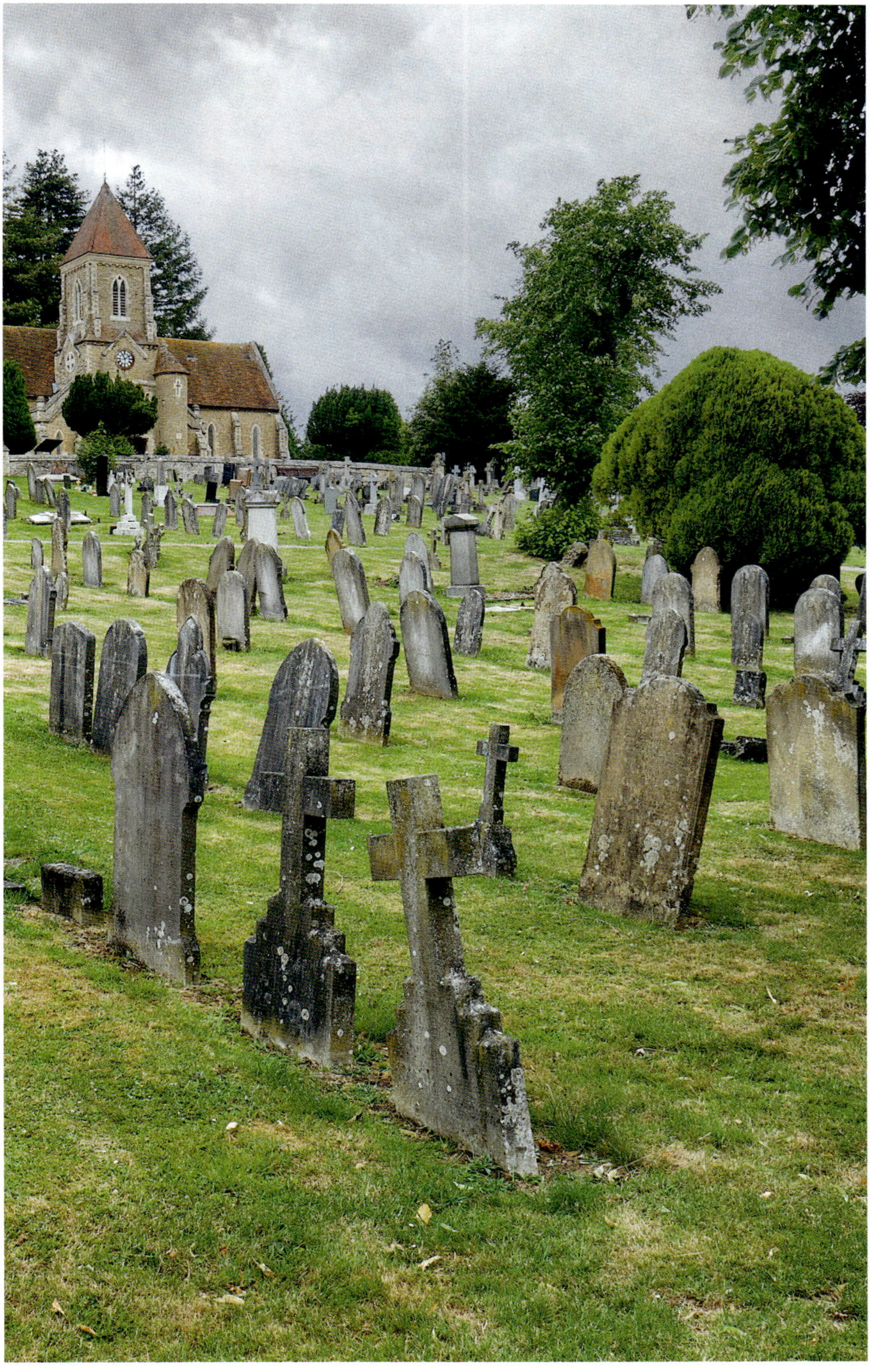

The Higgins Museum
Bedford

Formerly three cultural venues, The Higgins Bedford opened in 2013 to house an art gallery, a museum and several outstanding collections under one roof. The complex of buildings it occupies includes the Higgins Brewery and family home, itself representing 200 years of local history.

The museum offers a vibrant programme of regularly changing exhibitions and has a wide variety of permanent displays covering the archaeological, social and natural history of the local area. In the Great Bedfordians Gallery you will learn about local people such as John Bunyan, the prison reformer John Howard and Mabel Barltrop, who founded the Panacea Society.

Collections include items of porcelain, jewellery and costume, together with works by the 19th century architect William Burges and the 20th century painter, illustrator and graphic artist, Edward Bawden.

Further Information

4

Castle Lane, Bedford, MK40 3XD.

www.thehigginsbedford.org.uk

Access: Talks, tours and ticketed events throughout the year. Wheelchair access to all levels.

What's Nearby: The Panacea Museum www.panaceamuseum.org

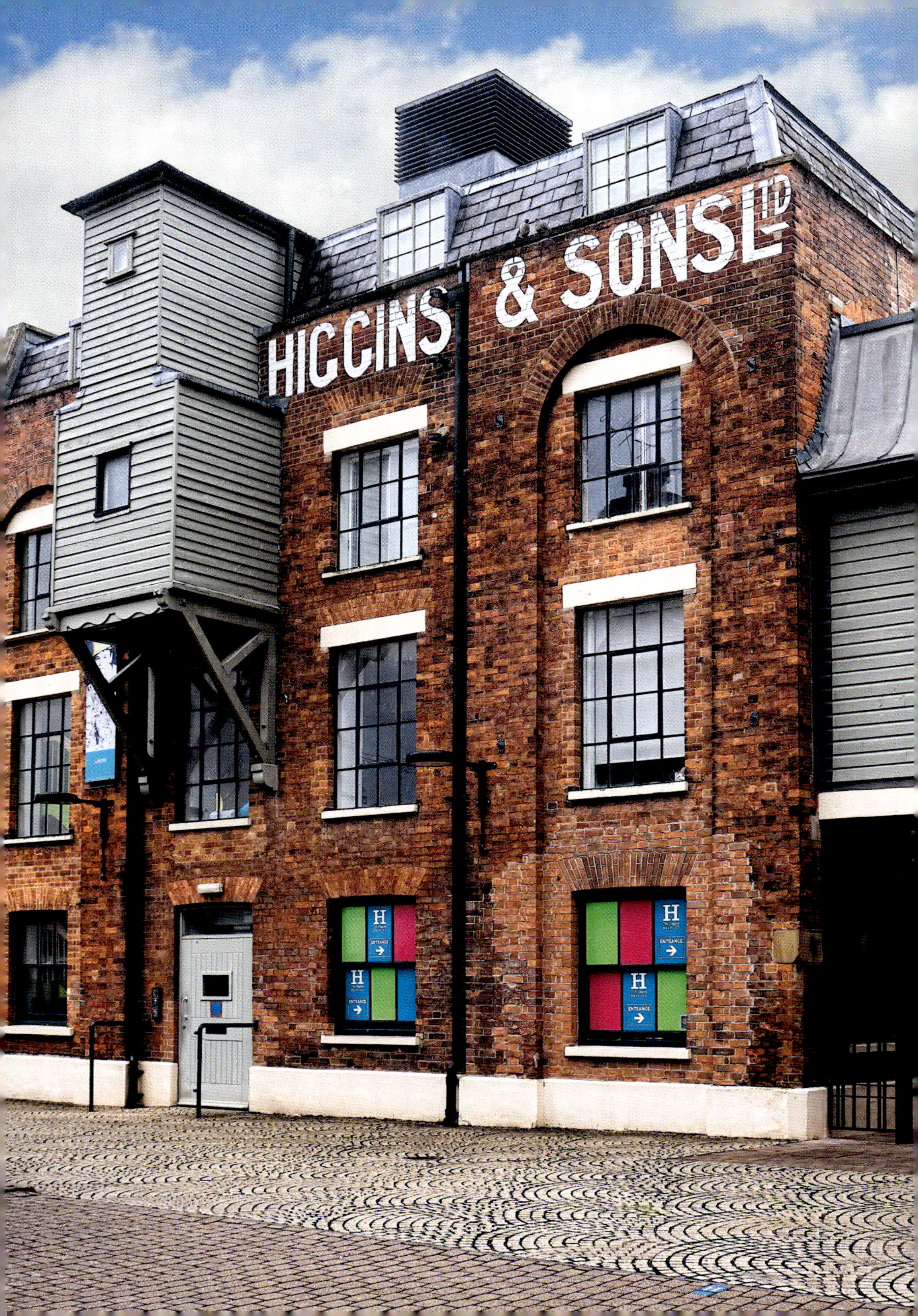
HIGGINS & SONS LTD
H
ENTRANCE

Bunyan Meeting House
Bedford

John Bunyan (1628-1688) was born in Elstow, just outside Bedford. He was arrested in November 1660 for preaching without the approval of the Anglican Church and sent to Bedford prison where he remained for twelve years. During his incarceration he wrote the world-famous *The Pilgrim's Progress*, a symbolic vision of a good man's pilgrimage through life. At one time it was second only to the Bible in popularity and has never been out of print.

The Bedford Meeting Church houses a museum to Bunyan and is well-known for its stained glass windows, in particular that of Bunyan in Bedford prison, quill in hand. In 1991, a Bedford couple sent a postcard of the window to Terry Waite, c/o Hezbollah, Party of God, Beirut, Lebanon, whilst he was held hostage. It arrived against the odds and he has recorded the comfort this gesture brought.

Further Information

5

Mill Street, Bedford, MK40 3EU.

www.bunyanmeeting.co.uk

What's Nearby: John Bunyan Trail
www.britishpilgrimage.org/portfolio/john-bunyan-trail

Image: © Courtesy of Paul Macro Photography.

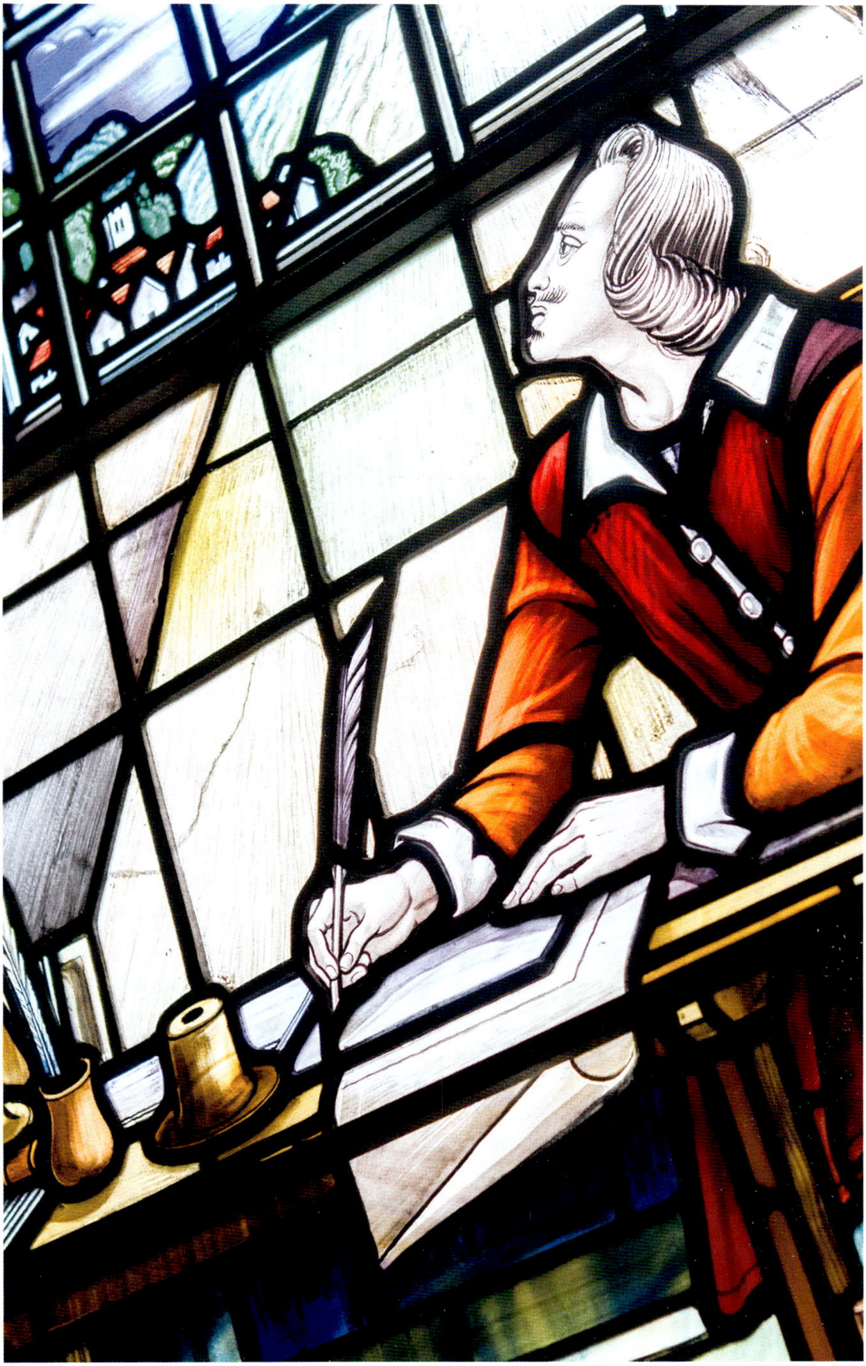

The Village of Elstow

Bedford

The historic village of Elstow, on the southern outskirts of Bedford, is the birthplace of John Bunyan and home to Elstow Abbey, founded by the Benedictines in the 11th century. Although altered over the centuries, it still retains six of its original Norman arches. Above the altar is a window celebrating Bunyan's greatest book, *The Pilgrim's Progress*. The small Bunyan chapel also features a memorial to those who suffered as prisoners of war in the Far East during World War II.

On the adjacent village green stands the Moot Hall, a 15th century timber-framed building containing both a courtroom and a market-house. The courtroom was in the main upper room, which was also used as a village meeting place, whilst the ground floor housed up to six shops.

Further Information

6

Church End, Elstow, Bedford , MK42 9XT.

www.elstow.weebly.com

The Moot Hall www.moothall.weebly.com

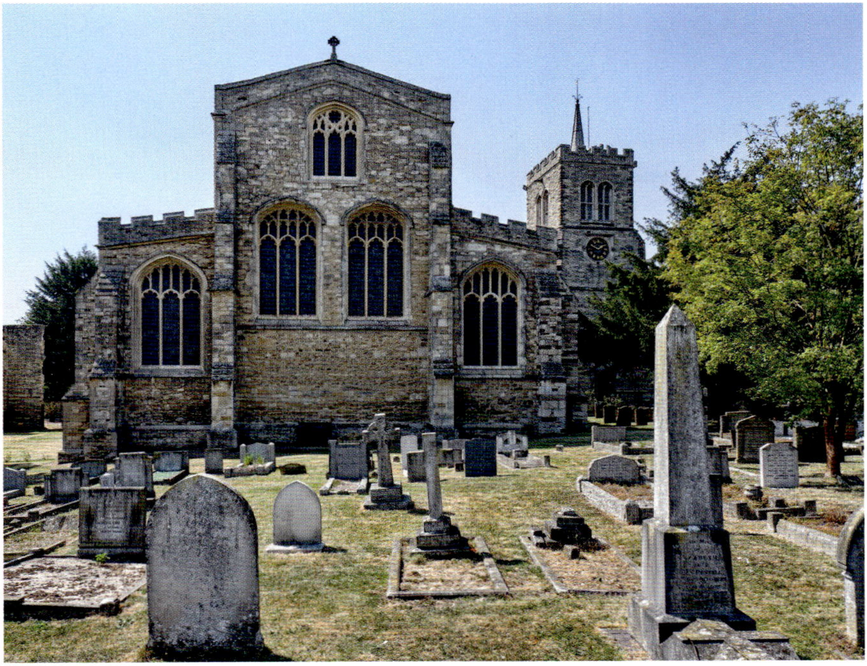

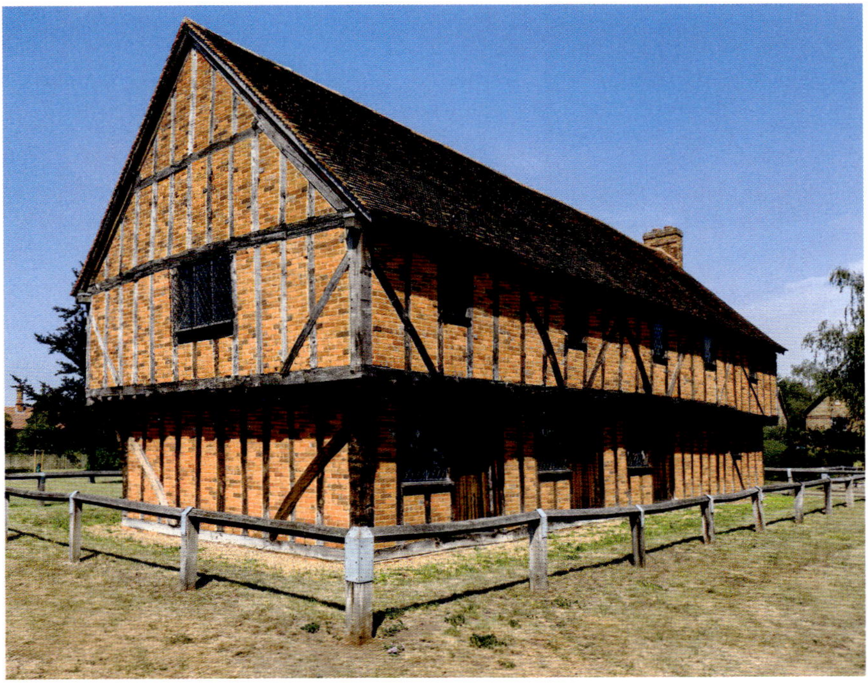

RSPB's The Lodge Nature Reserve and Gardens

Sandy

The Lodge is brimming with wildlife and heritage. Its five miles of paths wind past beautifully managed gardens, Iron Age banks and ditches, and quarry pits which paint a picture of Sandy's geological history.

In the spring you will be greeted with carpets of bluebells and drumming woodpeckers, while in the summer you might see common lizards basking with their young, or hobbies on the hunt for dragonflies over the heath. The autumn sees the forest floor come alive with about 600 species of fungus, while winter berries attract entire flocks of redwings.

The Lodge building itself was built in 1870 by the then Speaker of the House of Commons. It was later offered to Princess Margaret before the RSPB bought it in 1961 and it has been their headquarters ever since.

Further Information

7

The Lodge, Potton Road, Sandy, SG19 2DL.

www.rspb.org.uk/reserves-and-events/reserves-a-z/the-lodge

Access: Please check website for opening hours, admission and parking fee.

Images: © Courtesy of Ben Andrew (CiT Images).

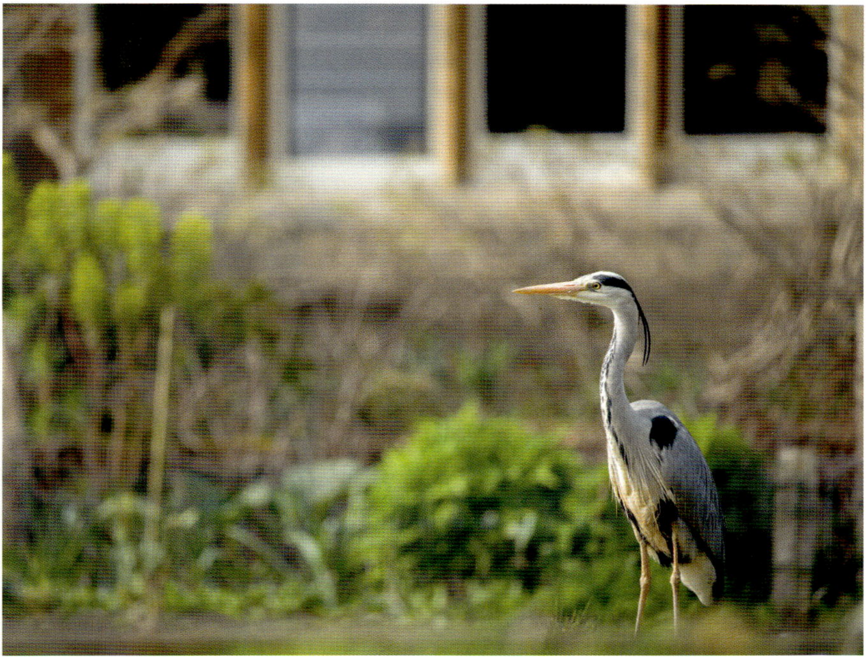

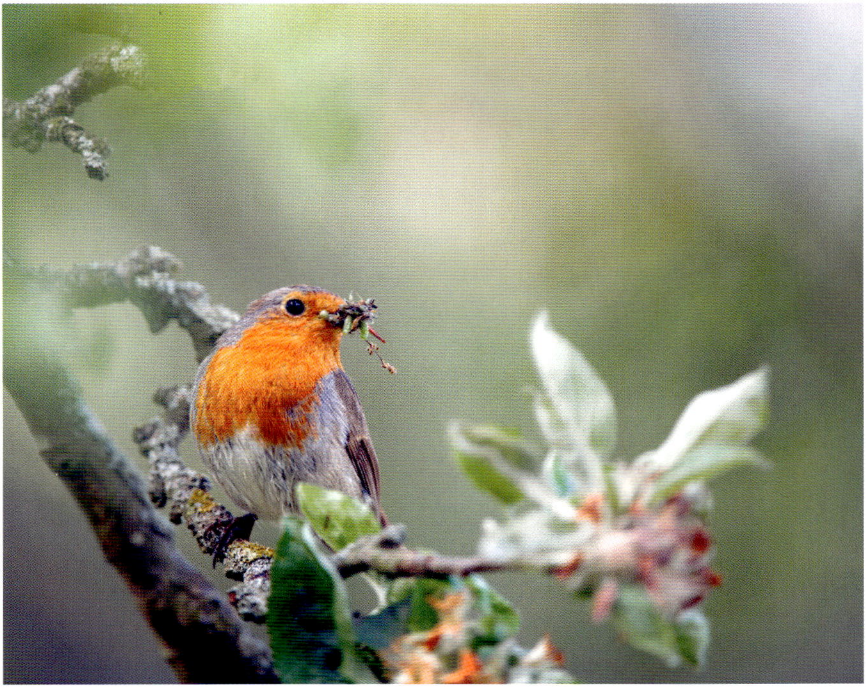

The Shuttleworth Collection and Swiss Garden

Old Warden

This venue offers the delightful contrast of a magnificent collection of industrial, agricultural and transport heritage exhibits with the relaxing, rather magical environment of the Swiss Garden, filled with seasonal colour.

Six large hangars showcase remarkable examples of early aviation, vintage vehicles, motorcycles and bicycles, including a penny farthing. This living and working museum is the legacy of Richard Ormonde Shuttleworth who died on an RAF training flight in 1940. His fascination with collecting a wide variety of mechanical objects formed the nucleus of the collection which can be seen today.

Visitors can also enjoy nearly 60 acres of parkland including a woodland sculpture trail, a lake, paddocks overlooking the grass airfield and the gentle hills of the North Park which afford fantastic views of Shuttleworth House and the surrounding countryside.

Further Information

8

Old Warden Aerodrome, Nr Biggleswade, SG18 9EP.

www.shuttleworth.org

What's Nearby: Queen Anne's Summerhouse
www.landmarktrust.org.uk/search-and-book/properties/queen-annes-summerhouse-13986
St. Leonard's Church
www.bedfordshireparishchurches.co.uk/wp/old-warden

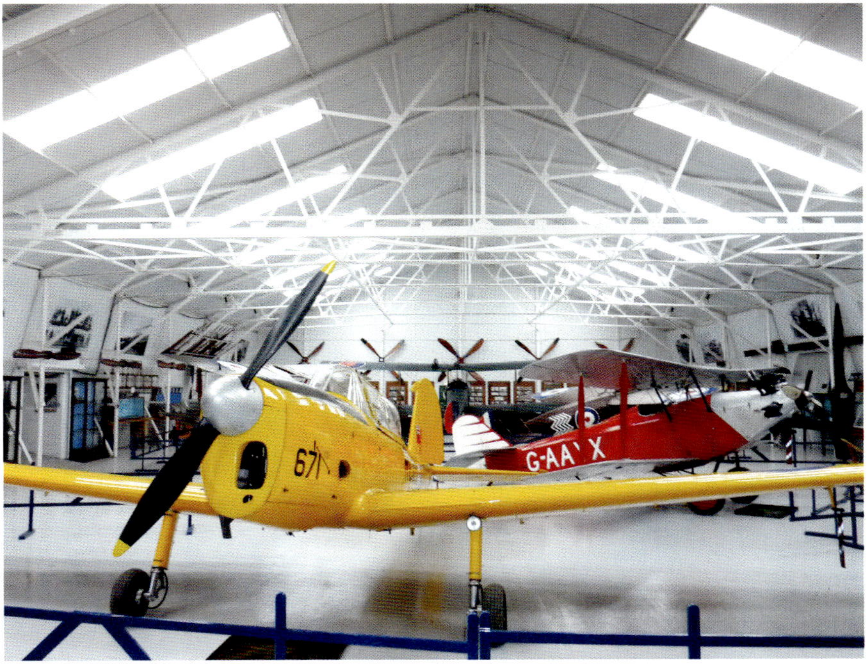

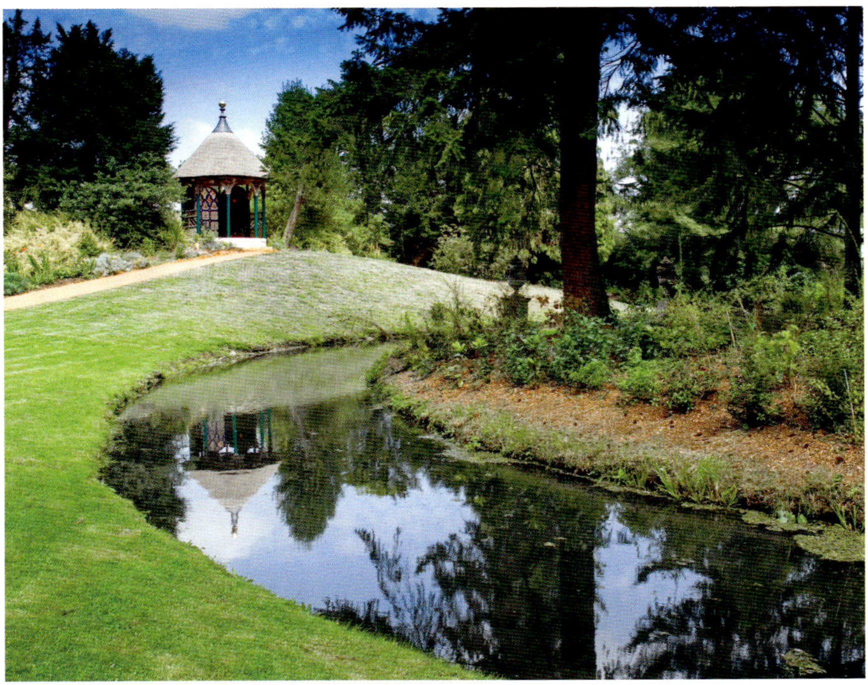

Jordans Mill

Broom

This historic Victorian flour mill, situated on the banks of the River Ivel, has been home to the Jordan family for 150 years. It is thought there has been a mill in this location for many centuries. Flour was produced here until 2000 when food production moved to a state-of-the-art factory.

The 19th century mill has been restored with a floor-to-ceiling glass screen dividing the working part from explanatory exhibition displays. Machinery has been restored to bring the milling process over the years to life and take visitors on a journey through time.

In the beautiful gardens outside the mill, cereals and crops of fruit and vegetables can be seen growing alongside ornamental flowers and plants. The extensive meadows and woodland offer a tranquil wildlife sanctuary.

Further Information

9

Holme Mills, Southill Road, Broom, SG18 9JX.

www.jordansmill.com

Access: Please check website for opening hours. Entrance is free but there may be a small charge for guided tours.

What's Nearby: Willington Dovecote.
www.nationaltrust.org.uk/willington-dovecote-and-stables

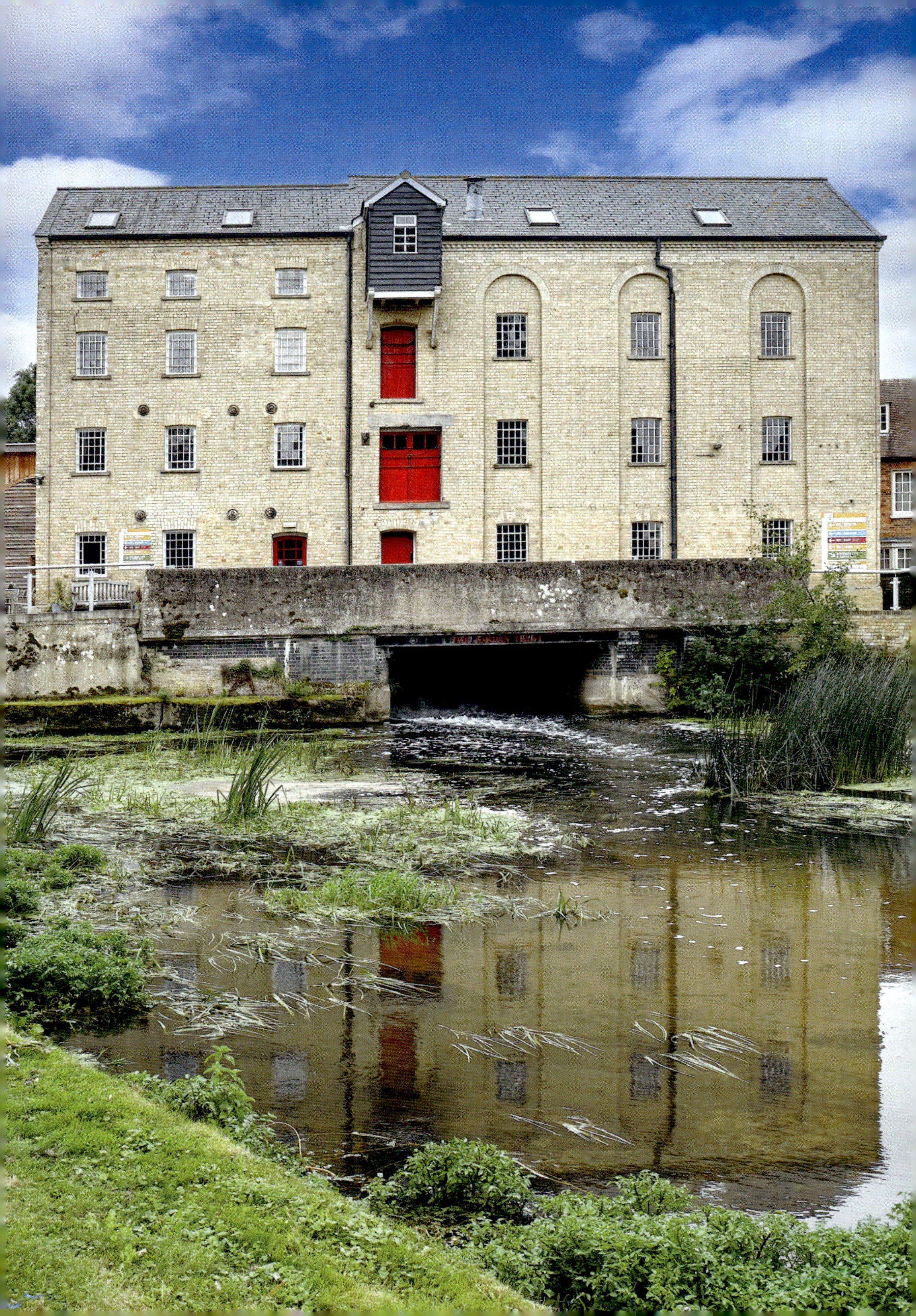

Stotfold Water Mill

Stotfold

A water mill is believed to have stood on this site beside the River Ivel for a thousand years. The present building, of special architectural and historical interest, is preserved and maintained as a working mill by Stotfold Water Mill Trust. The Trust also manages the adjacent Stotfold Nature Reserve to promote public appreciation of the flora and fauna to be found here.

The 4.2 metre wide overshot corn mill waterwheel is the widest in the country. The power this generates drives the mill wheel. On display is a remnant of the original upright shaft and the diesel engine used to power the mill machinery in the early 1950s. Visitors are offered an insight into the milling process and the history of the mill and can even see demonstrations of the grinding process.

Further Information

10

Mill Lane, Stotfold, SG5 4NU.

www.stotfoldmill.com

Access: Nature reserve open all year round. Please check website for mill, shop and tea room opening times.

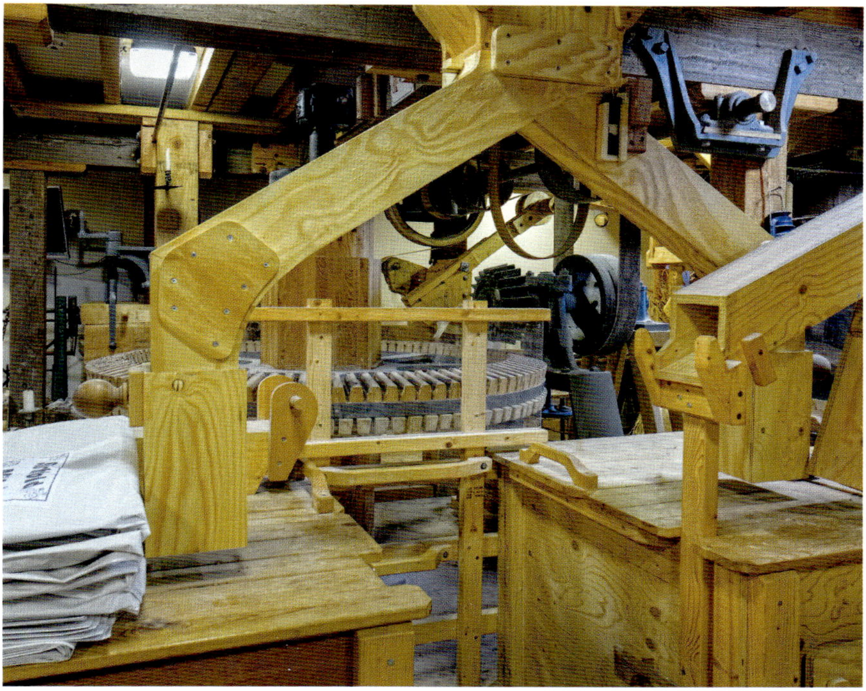

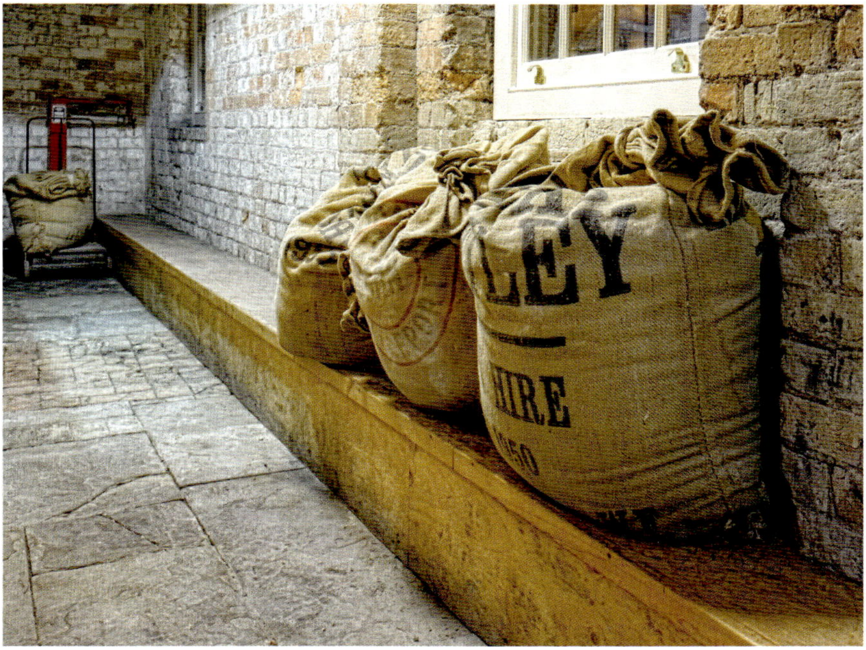
LEY
HIRE

Chicksands Priory
Shefford

Chicksands Priory is a Grade 1 listed Ancient Monument which now serves as an Officers' Mess for a large MoD base. Founded in the 12th century, it was the third largest Gilbertine Priory and the only house of this purely English monastic order to be founded during the lifetime of St. Gilbert outside his own county of Lincolnshire.

After the Dissolution, in 1576, the priory passed to the Osborn family and remained in their possession until 1936, when Sir Algernon Osborn, 7th Baronet, sold it to the Commissioners for Crown Lands. In 1939 it became RAF Chicksands Priory and in 1941 it served as a communications centre and an intercept facility. The USAF joined the RAF base in 1950 and moved out in 1995, after which the priory was restored to its present condition.

Further Information

11

Chicksands, Shefford, SG17 5QB.

www.chicksandspriory.co.uk

Access: By appointment only. Details can be found via the website.

What's Nearby: The Military Intelligence Museum.
www.militaryintelligencemuseum.org

Image: © Courtesy of Clive Larrett.

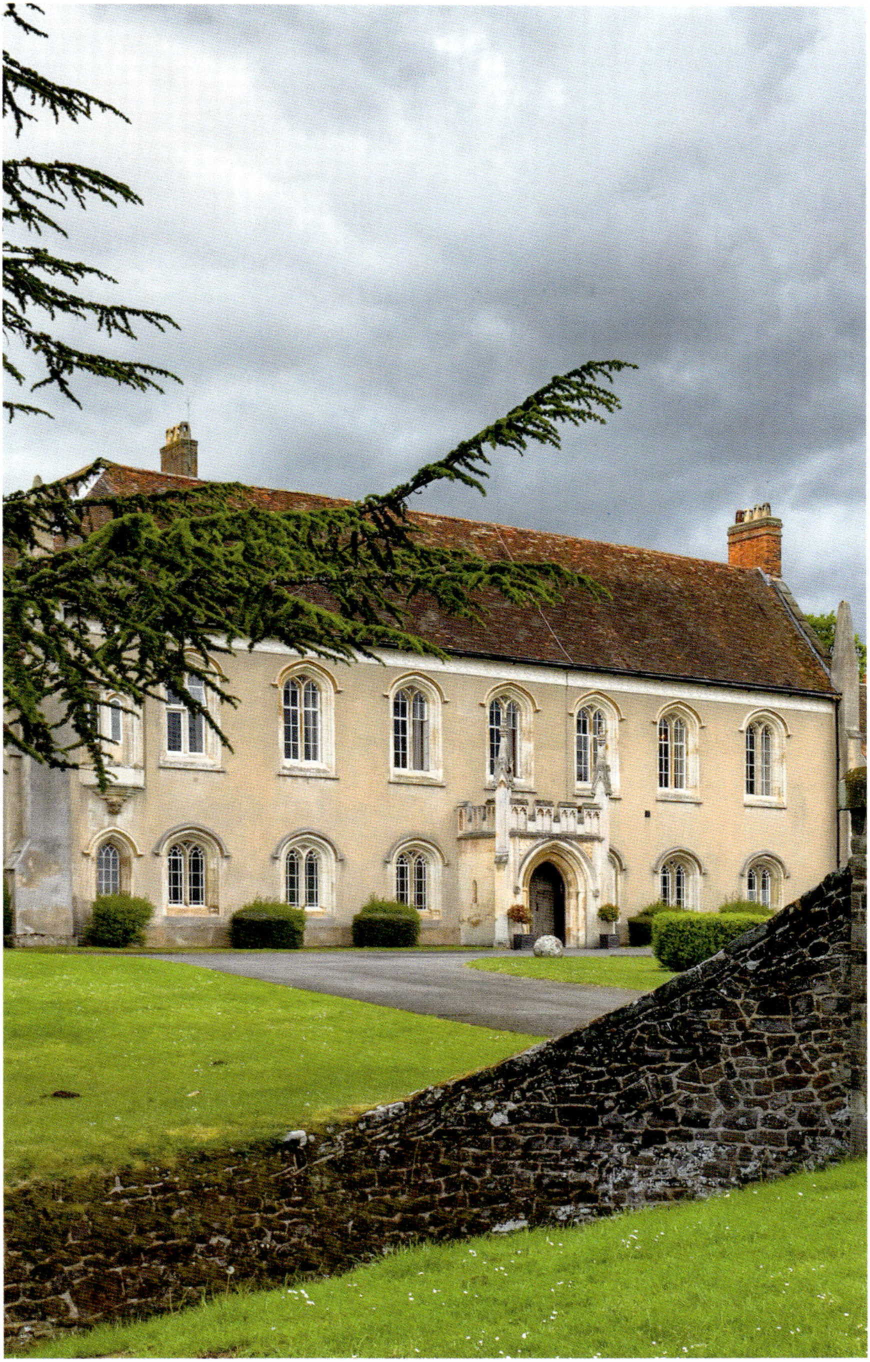

St. Mary the Virgin

Marston Moretaine

St. Mary's is a fine example of a medieval parish church with many notable treasures. The structure principally dates from the mid-15th century, with a nave believed to have been built by Thomas Reynes, the last of the Moreteyne family to hold the Manor of Marston. The vestry, with a priest's room above it, and the chancel are believed to date from the 14th century. Of particular interest are the remarkable *Last Judgement* Doom painting above the chancel arch and the marble tomb of Sir Thomas Snagge, MP and Speaker of the House under Elizabeth I.

Although not unique, the detached tower is often the subject of curiosity. The thick base walls indicate the structure predates the main building and some suggest it proves the presence of a fortified structure from before the Norman Conquest.

Further Information

12

Church Walk, Marston Moretaine, MK43 0NA.

www.stmarysmarston.org

Access: Generally open daily.

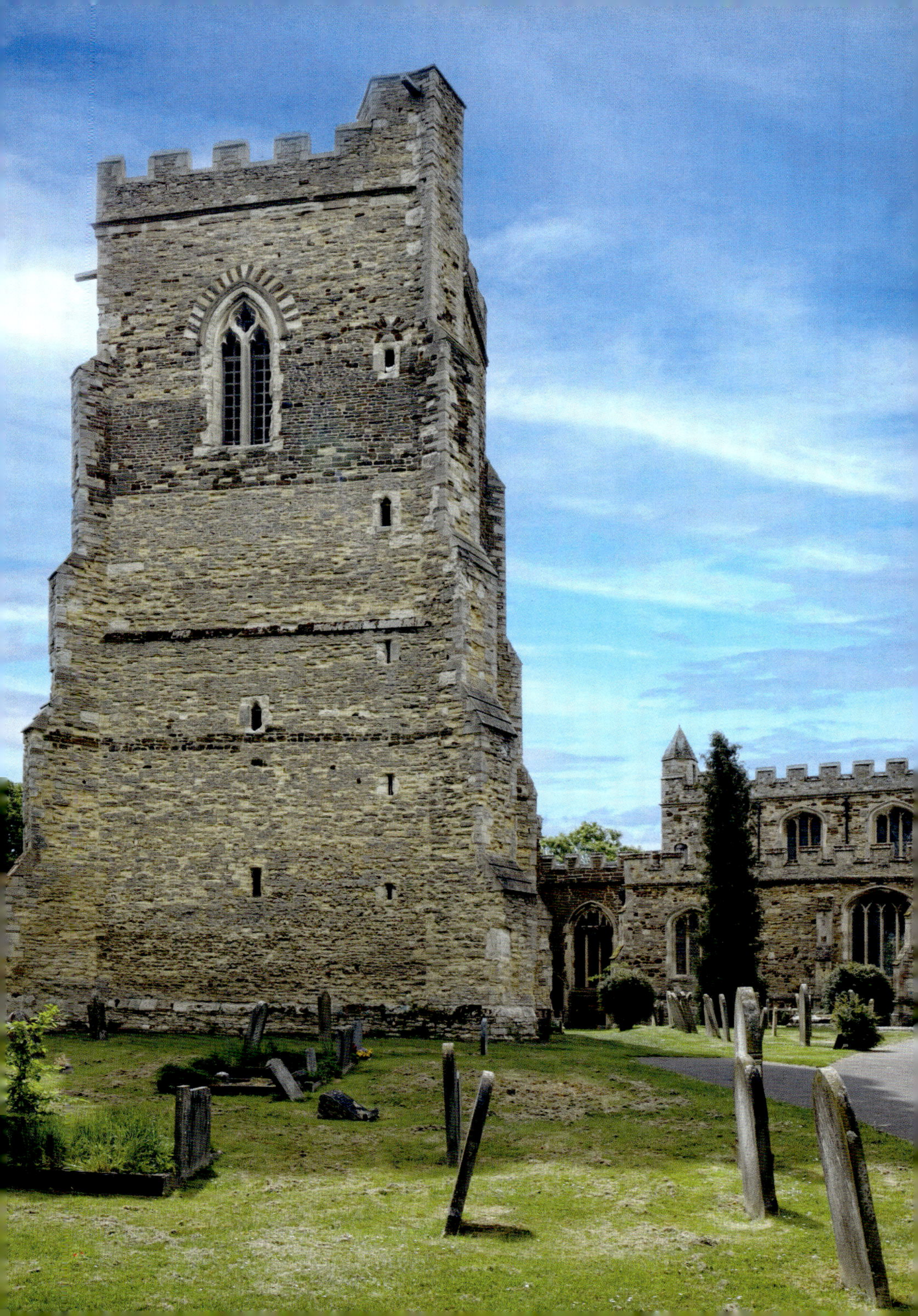

Wrest Park
Silsoe

Discover over 90 acres of beautiful gardens showcasing French, Dutch, Italian and English styles. Explore landscapes and woodland walks with over 40 statues dotted around the grounds which include an ornate marble fountain, the 18th century Bowling Green House and a Chinese temple and bridge. The French design of the 19th century Orangery is of notable architectural interest whilst walkways alongside the Long Water lead to a spectacular pavilion built by Baroque architect Thomas Archer.

The Dairy Sculpture Gallery showcases some of the estate's most beautiful statues restored to their former glory. The Archaeological Collections Store contains a treasure trove of unique and special objects spanning 2,000 years of England's history.

The French Room contains the stunning 'Eldorado' wallpapers and intricate hand-painted papers can be seen in the Chinese Room.

Further Information

13

Silsoe, MK45 4HR.

www.english-heritage.org.uk/visit/places/wrest-park

Access: Please check the website as some areas are only accessible on selected days.
Entry fee applies.

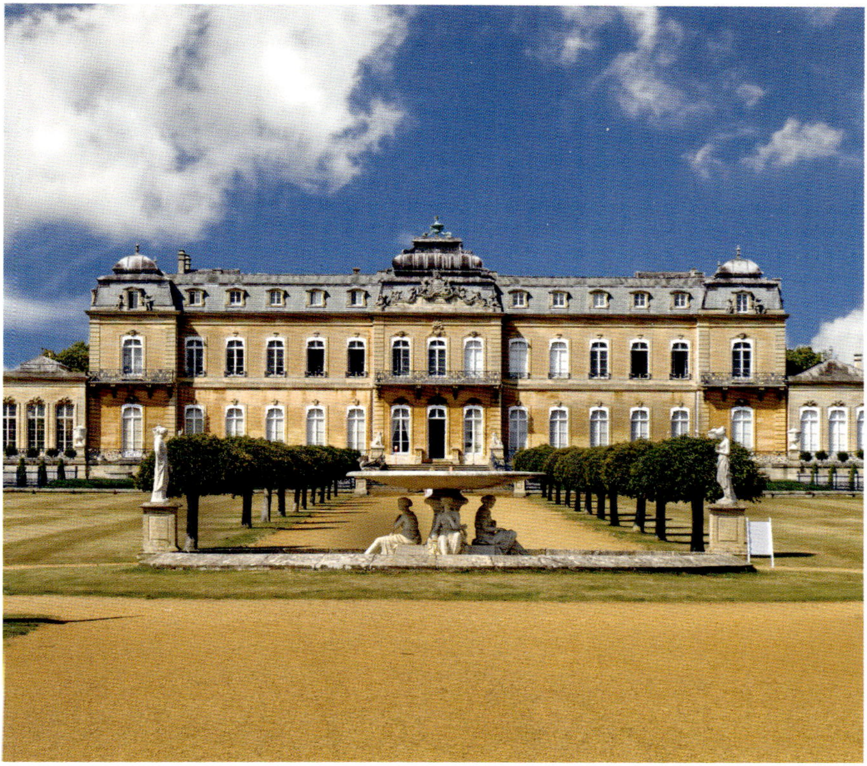

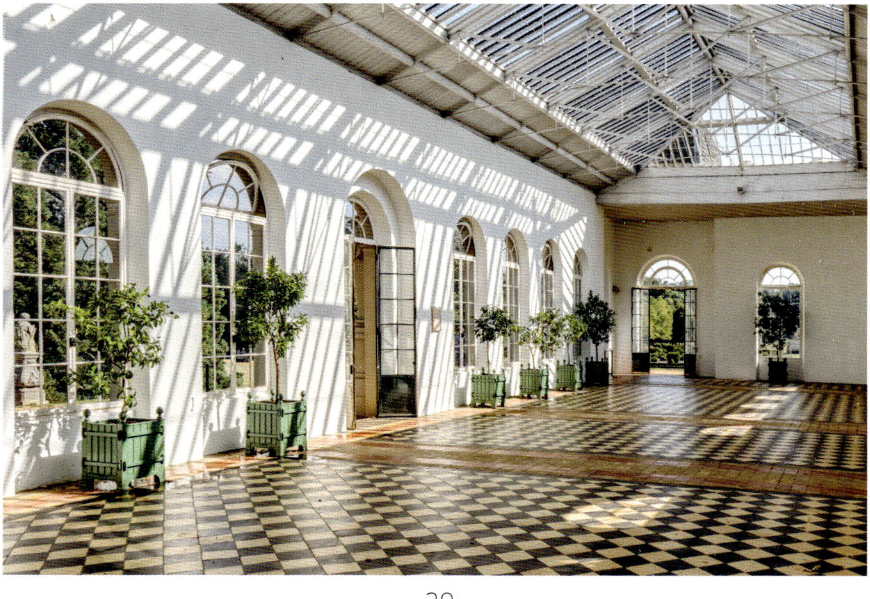

De Grey Mausoleum
Flitton

The De Grey Mausoleum is attached to the mid-15th century parish church of St. John at Flitton. Henry Grey, 1st Duke of Kent, developed the original chapel, built around 1605, into a large cruciform shaped mausoleum. The work took 5 years, finishing in 1710, and was intended as a burial place to reflect the growing status of his family and descendants.

Family members were buried in vaults beneath the stone floor marked by one of the finest collections of monument effigies in England. These monuments display styles spanning three centuries including late Gothic, Jacobean, Baroque, Neo-Classical and Neo-Gothic.

A superbly sculpted Baroque monument, attributed to the Flemish sculptor John Michael Rysbrack (1694-1770), over the resting place of Henry Grey and his two wives, is probably the finest piece in the collection.

Further Information

14

High Street, Flitton, MK45 5EJ.

www.english-heritage.org.uk/visit/places/de-grey-mausoleum-flitton

Access: Free entry but access is limited to certain days in certain months - please check website for details.

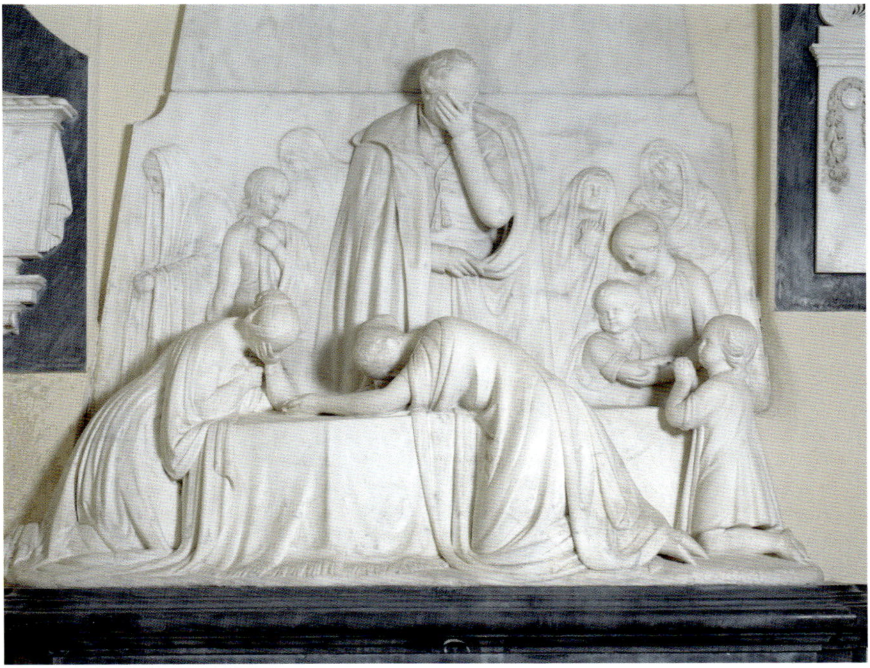

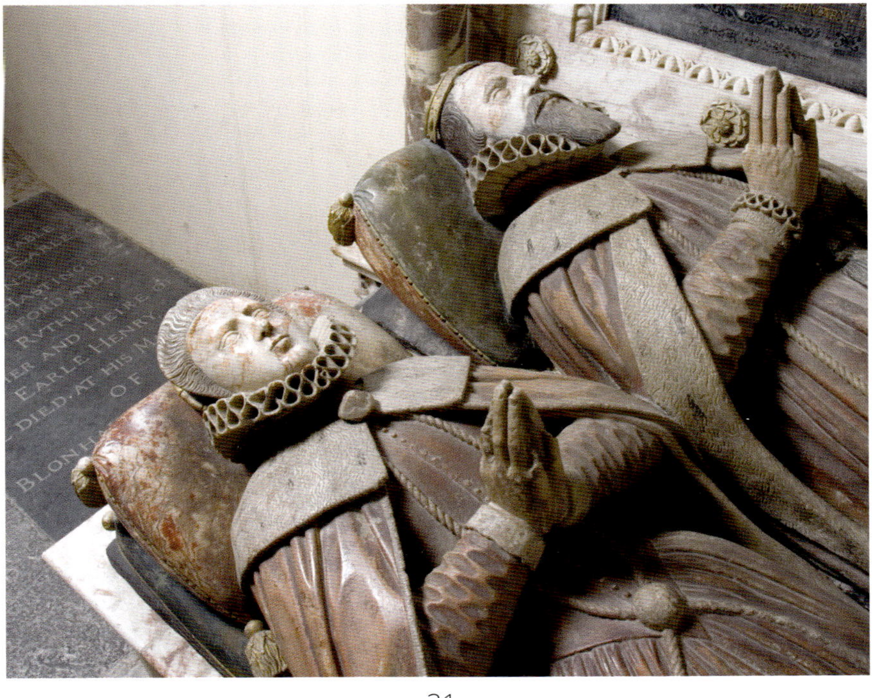
RVTHIN
ER AND HEIRE
EARLE HENRY
DIED AT HIS
OF

Woburn Abbey

Woburn

Woburn Abbey has been the home of the Earls and Dukes of Bedford, one of England's most powerful families, since the 1620s. It has been at the centre of social and political history including everything from political reform, royal state visits, imprisonment, beheading, grand tours and love affairs.

The Abbey houses an outstanding art work collection including the largest private collection of Venetian views by Canaletto on public view, the *Armada Portrait* of Queen Elizabeth I, as well as works by Gainsborough, Rembrandt, Reynolds, Van Dyck, Queen Victoria and Richard Stone.

Splendid rooms include a unique grotto which dates from the 1630s, state apartments with original 18th century architecture and underground vaults containing the family's gold and silver collection. The Holland Library houses one of the largest private collections of natural history books.

Further Information

15

London Road, Woburn, MK17 9WA.

www.woburnabbey.co.uk

Woburn Chinese Dairy.
www.historicengland.org.uk/listing/the-list/list-entry/1321667

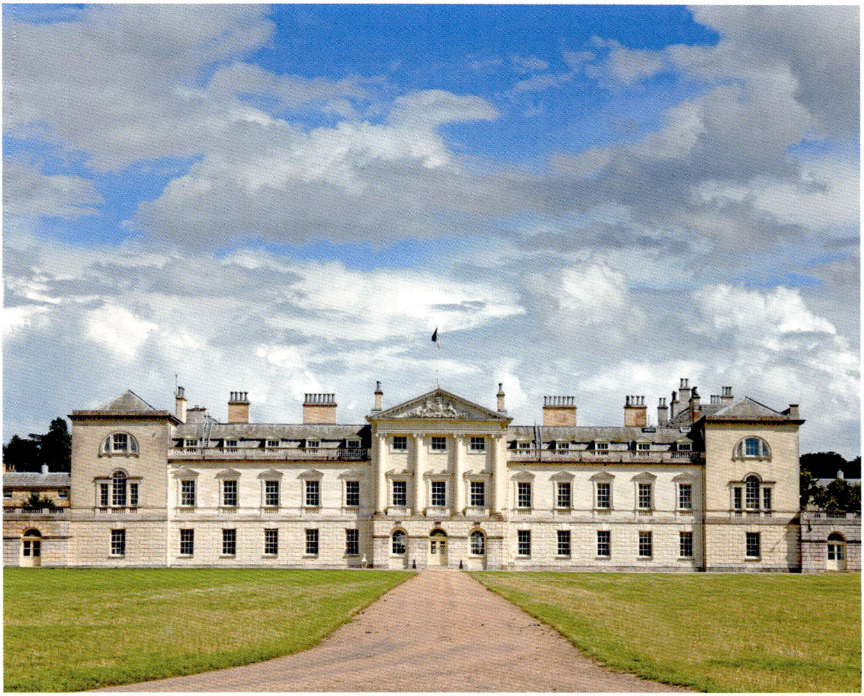

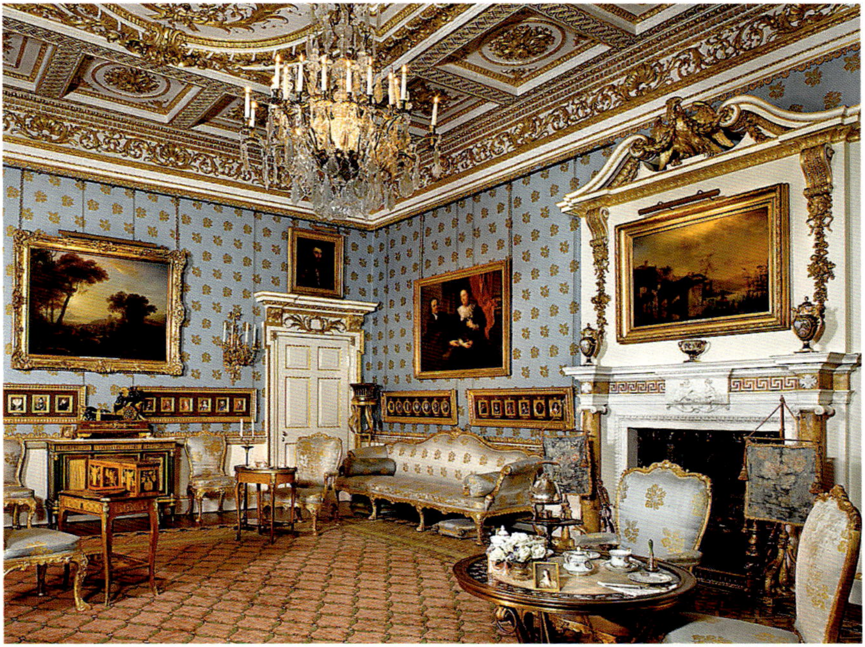

Totternhoe Knolls

Totternhoe

Totternhoe Knolls are a very different 'treasure' and are part of the Chilterns Area of Outstanding Natural Beauty. Depending on the time of year butterflies, orchids and a plethora of wild flowers abound in this Site of Special Scientific Interest which lies on chalk downs and covers over 32 acres of delightful English countryside.

The site includes Totternhoe Castle, probably built in the late 11th century. Only the earthworks survive, with a mound five metres tall and 40 metres wide. It is unusual in having three baileys.

Part of the site was formerly a quarry for Totternhoe Stone, highly valued for decorative work, and which is widely found in the region's churches and in buildings further afield such as Westminster Abbey and Windsor Castle.

Circular walks from the car park take in magnificent views of Bedfordshire.

Further Information

16

Castle Hill Road, Totternhoe, Dunstable, LU6 1QG.

www.chilternsociety.org.uk/?s=totternhoe+knolls

Access: See website for details of a wide range of walks and cycle routes and their difficulty levels.

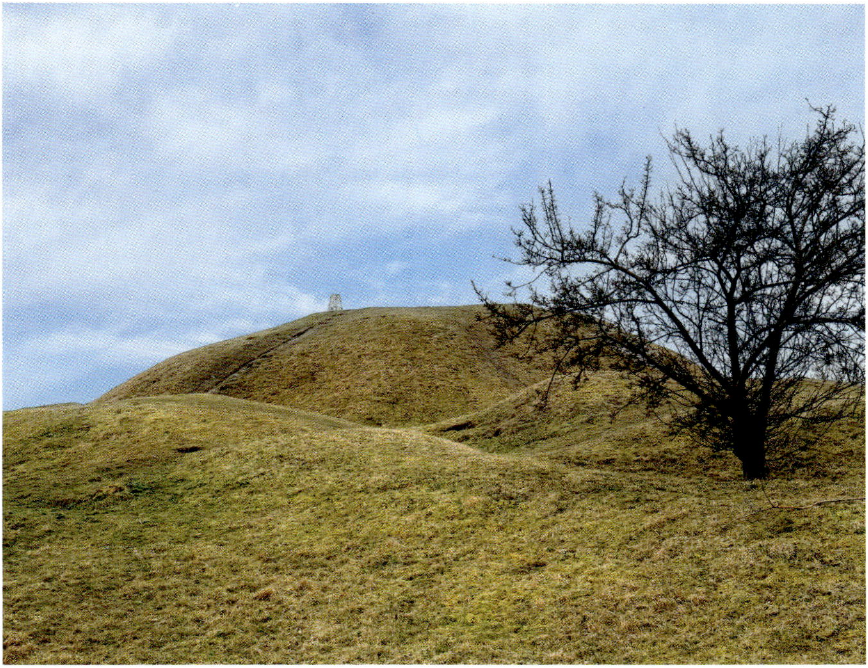

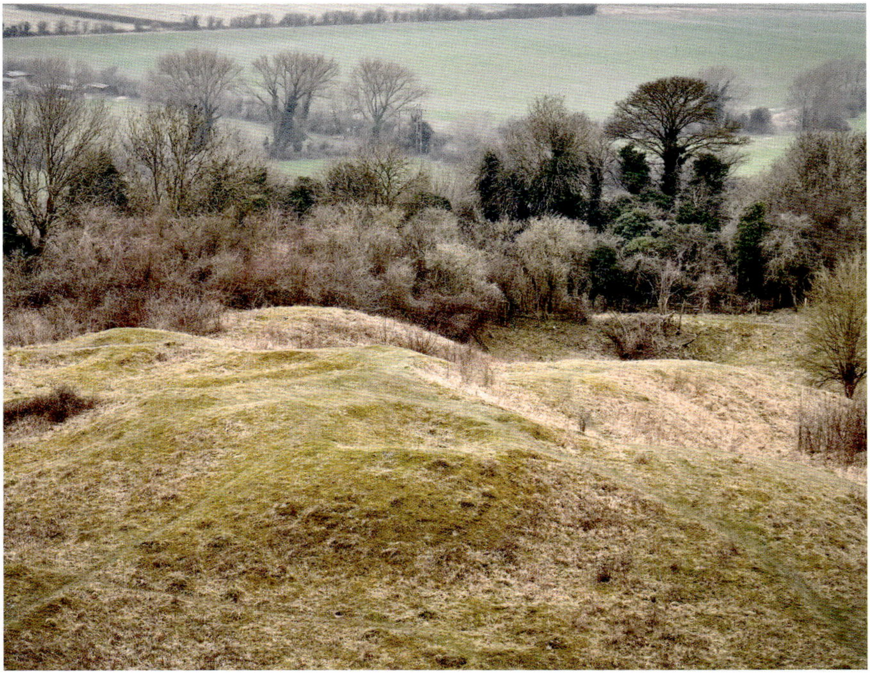

Priory Church of St. Peter
Dunstable

St. Peter's is one of the best examples of Norman architecture in England. It is all that remains of the Augustinian Priory founded in the 1120s by Henry I.

In 1190, Queen Eleanor's coffin rested here overnight on its way to Westminster Abbey.

In 1533, St. Peter's was the site of the court at which Archbishop Cranmer and the bishops decreed that Henry VIII and Catherine of Aragon had never been legally married. Shortly afterwards, in 1540, the Priory was dissolved. The priory church survived several tumultuous centuries, as witnessed by the shot marks on the old west doors fired during the English Civil War, until it received substantial restoration in the 20th century.

Highlights of the church include the intricate 14th century screen, with five open bays, and the Fayrey Pall, a 15th century embroidered cloth.

Further Information

17

Church Close, Dunstable, LU5 4RS.

www.dunstableparish.org.uk/priory-church

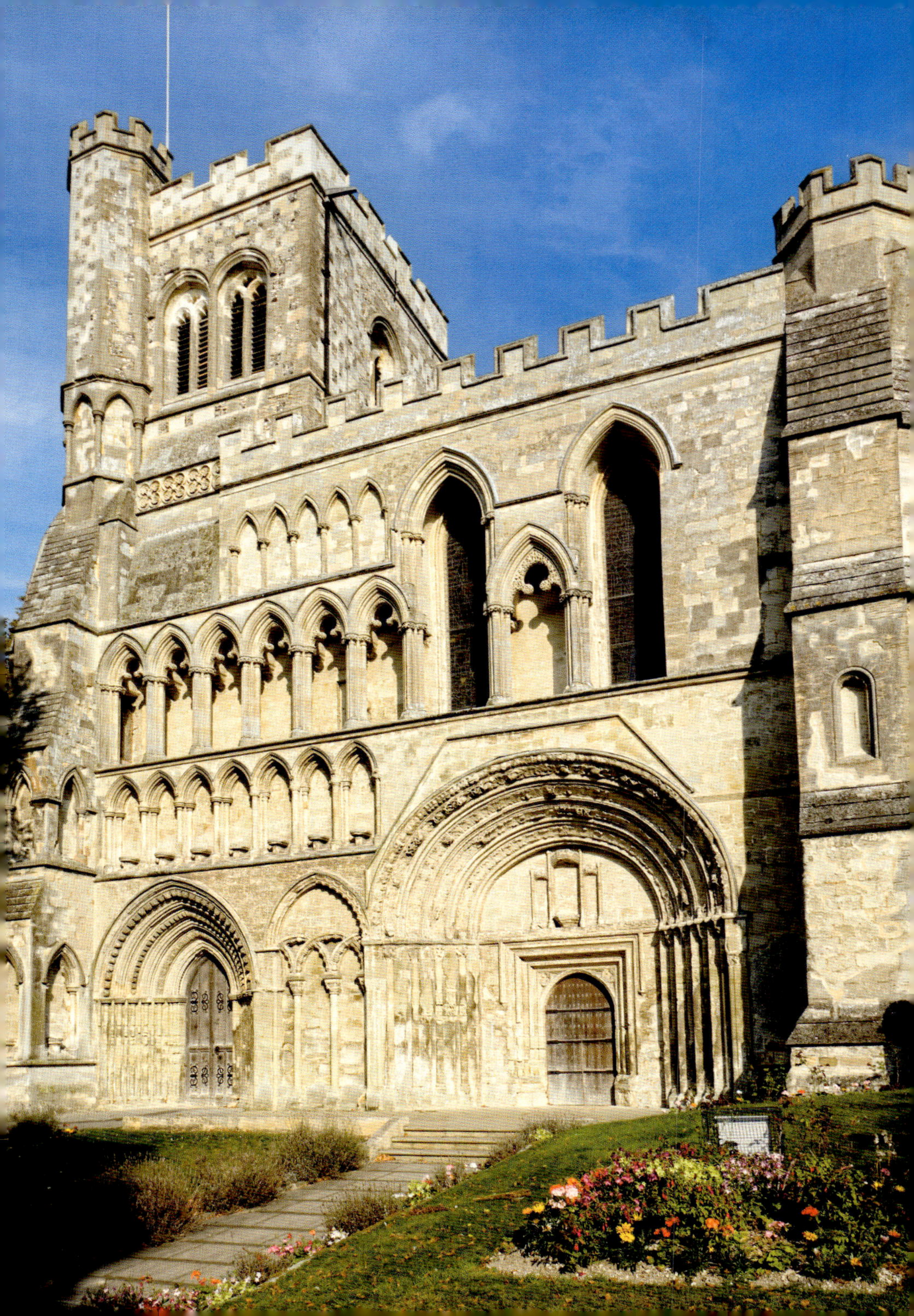

Tree Cathedral
Whipsnade

This is a very different sort of Cathedral. It was conceived in the 1930s as an act of 'Faith, Hope and Reconciliation' by Edmund Blyth to honour close colleagues killed towards the end of World War I. Inspired by the construction of Liverpool Anglican Cathedral, he began planting trees and shrubs to represent the shape of a cathedral, thus creating a unique and lasting legacy to his fallen comrades. Work was suspended during World War II but by 1952 there had been sufficient progress to allow the commencement of annual ecumenical services.

This beautifully maintained site was donated to the National Trust in 1960 and awarded a Grade II listing by Historic England in 2017. Visitors to this tranquil green space can identify distinct areas including a nave, transepts, a chancel, cloisters and chapels, delineated by different varieties of tree.

Further Information

18

Whipsnade, Dunstable, LU6 2LQ.

www.nationaltrust.org.uk/whipsnade-tree-cathedral

Access: Open daily. Limited parking.

What's Nearby: Giant Hillside Chalk Lion.
Visible from the B489 Aylesbury to Dunstable road.
www.lonelyplanet.com/articles/hillside-chalk-lion-whipsnade-zoo

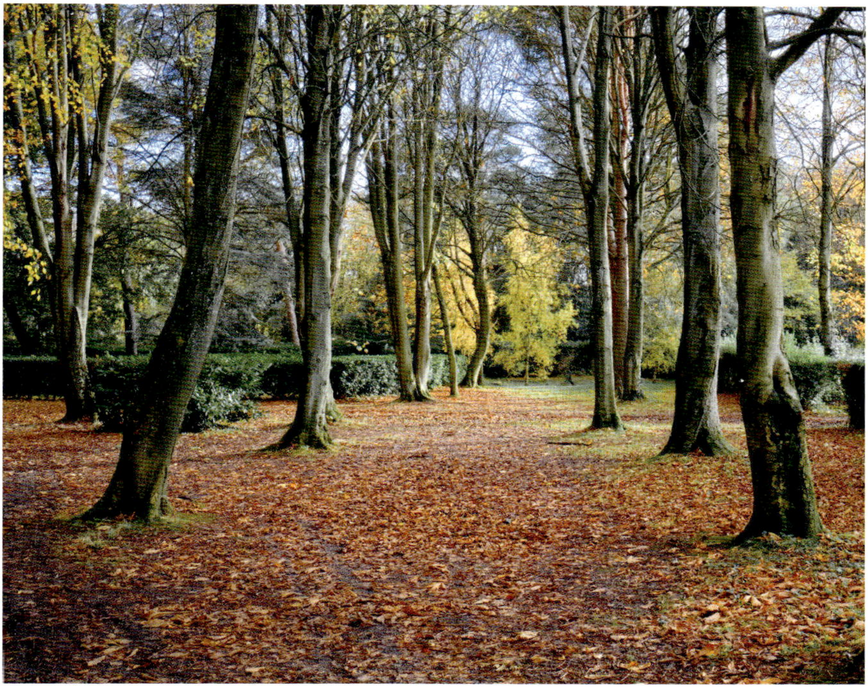

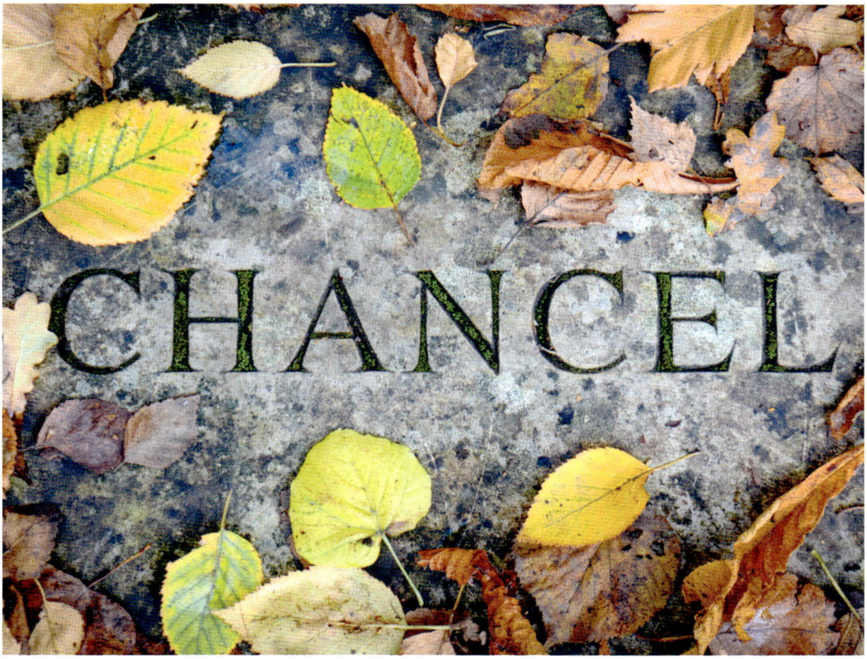
CHANCEL

Stockwood Discovery Centre
Luton

This is a perfect free entry, family day out featuring the largest carriage collection in Europe, interactive special exhibitions, an outdoor children's play area and beautiful gardens laid out in a variety of styles, inspired by centuries of gardening history.

Acclaimed artist Ian Hamilton Finlay's sculptures form an integral part of the classical 'Improvement Garden'. Recently developed areas include a sensory garden and a medicinal garden, designed along environmentally sustainable principles.

The museum galleries bring the stories of local people to life, dating from prehistoric times to the present day, particularly through displays of local archaeology, rural crafts and trades. The 15th century *Wenlock Jug* is a rare medieval bronze masterpiece and there are believed to be only two similar items still existing in the UK.

Further Information

19

London Road, Luton, LU1 4LX.

www.culturetrust.com/venues/stockwood-discovery-centre

What's Nearby: Wardown House Museum & Gallery.
www.culturetrust.com/venues/wardown-house-museum-gallery

Images: © Courtesy of Greta Zabulyte/Stockwood Discovery Centre.

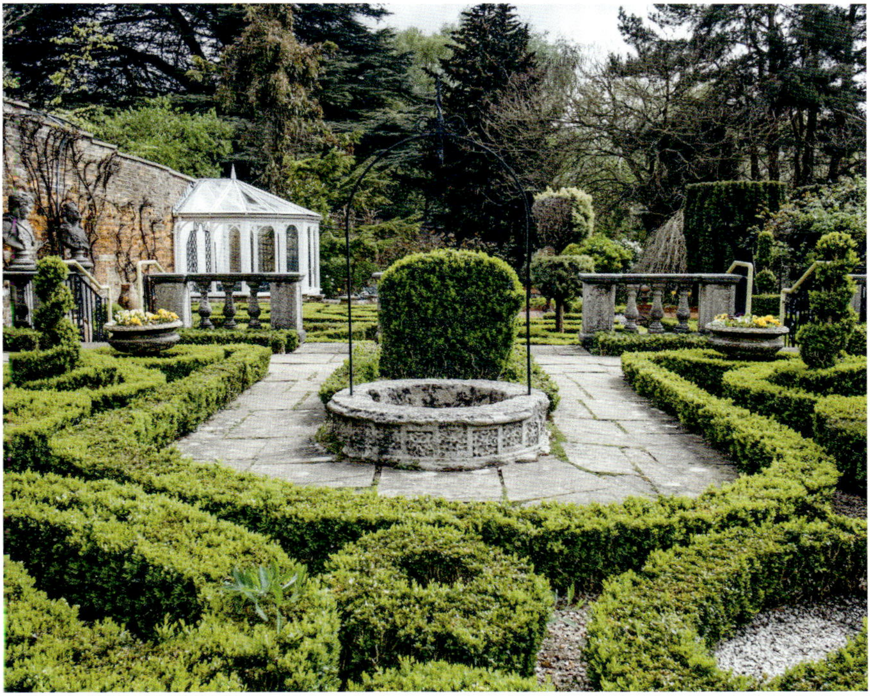

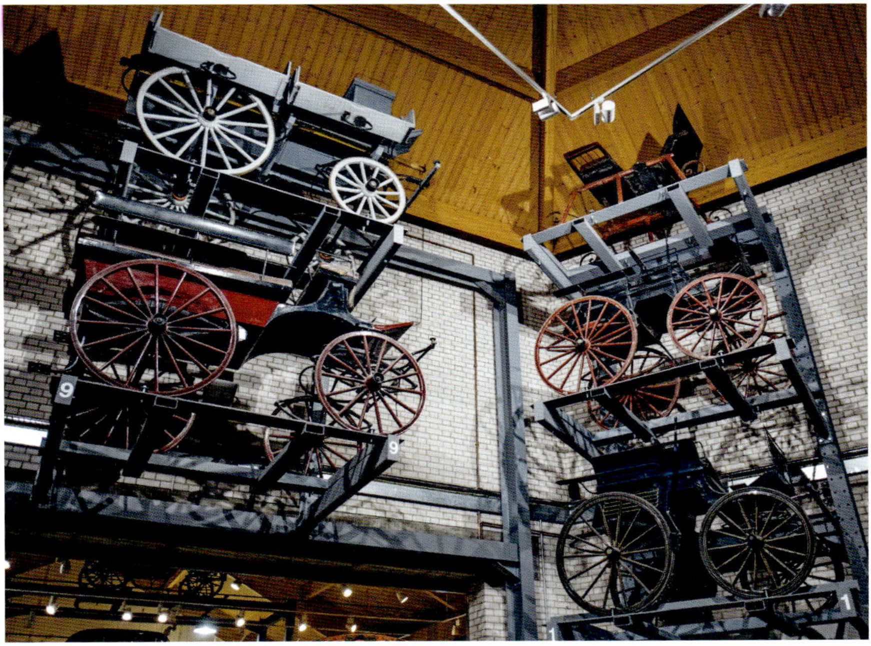

Luton Hoo Estate Walled Garden

Luton

This garden was designed by Capability Brown in the late 1760s. It evolved to match the fashion of horticulture in the 19th and 20th centuries but fell into decline in the late 1980s, becoming dilapidated and unmanaged. In 2001 a volunteer team, including Heritage Volunteers from TAS Harpenden Area, set about its recovery.

Today the site comprises a five-acre garden surrounded by the 18th century octagonal wall, a range of glass houses, including a timber-framed Mackenzie Moncur conservatory dated circa 1908, a peach house and a vinery.

There is also a selection of rare service buildings surrounding the garden including the Head Gardener's office, a potting shed, a boiler house, stables and propagation houses. The garden continues to be revived, repaired and re-imagined for the enjoyment of all.

Further Information

20

Farm Rd, Luton, LU1 4LF.

www.lutonhooestate.co.uk/walled-garden

Access: Check for limited opening hours.

Images: © Courtesy of Torben Cox.

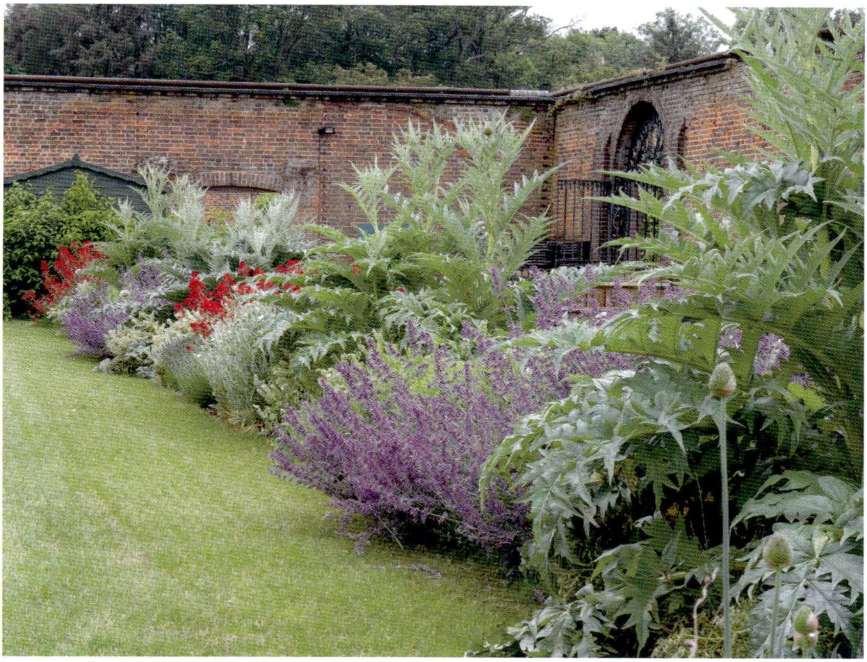

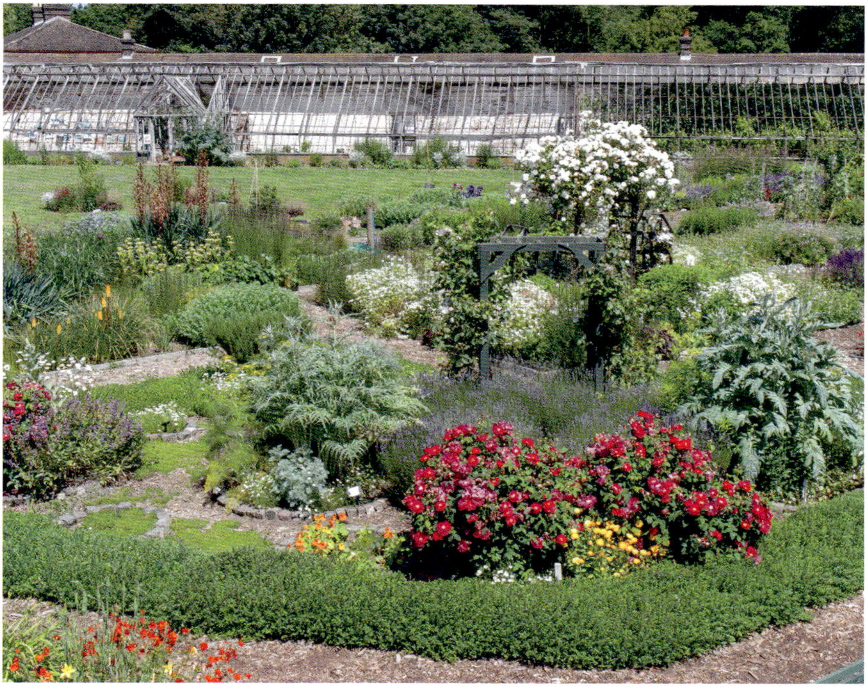

Royston Cave

Royston

Royston Cave is an enigma. No records of its age or purpose exist. Some theories suggest it was used by the Knights Templar, others as a private chapel or hermitage. Discovered by accident in 1742, Royston Cave is man-made and beehive shaped, cut 8m into the chalk that underlies Royston's ancient crossroads, Ermine Street and Icknield Way. The contents of the cave included a human skull and fragments of a drinking vessel.

The cave is decorated with extensive low relief wall carvings. The carvings are mostly Christian in depiction and medieval in style. They include representations of the Crucifixion and notable saints such as St. Katherine and St. Christopher. Elsewhere are figures of a horse and an Earth Goddess, believed to be pagan fertility symbols.

Further Information

21

Melbourn Street, Royston, SG8 7BZ.

www.roystoncave.co.uk

Image: © Courtesy of Royston Cave.

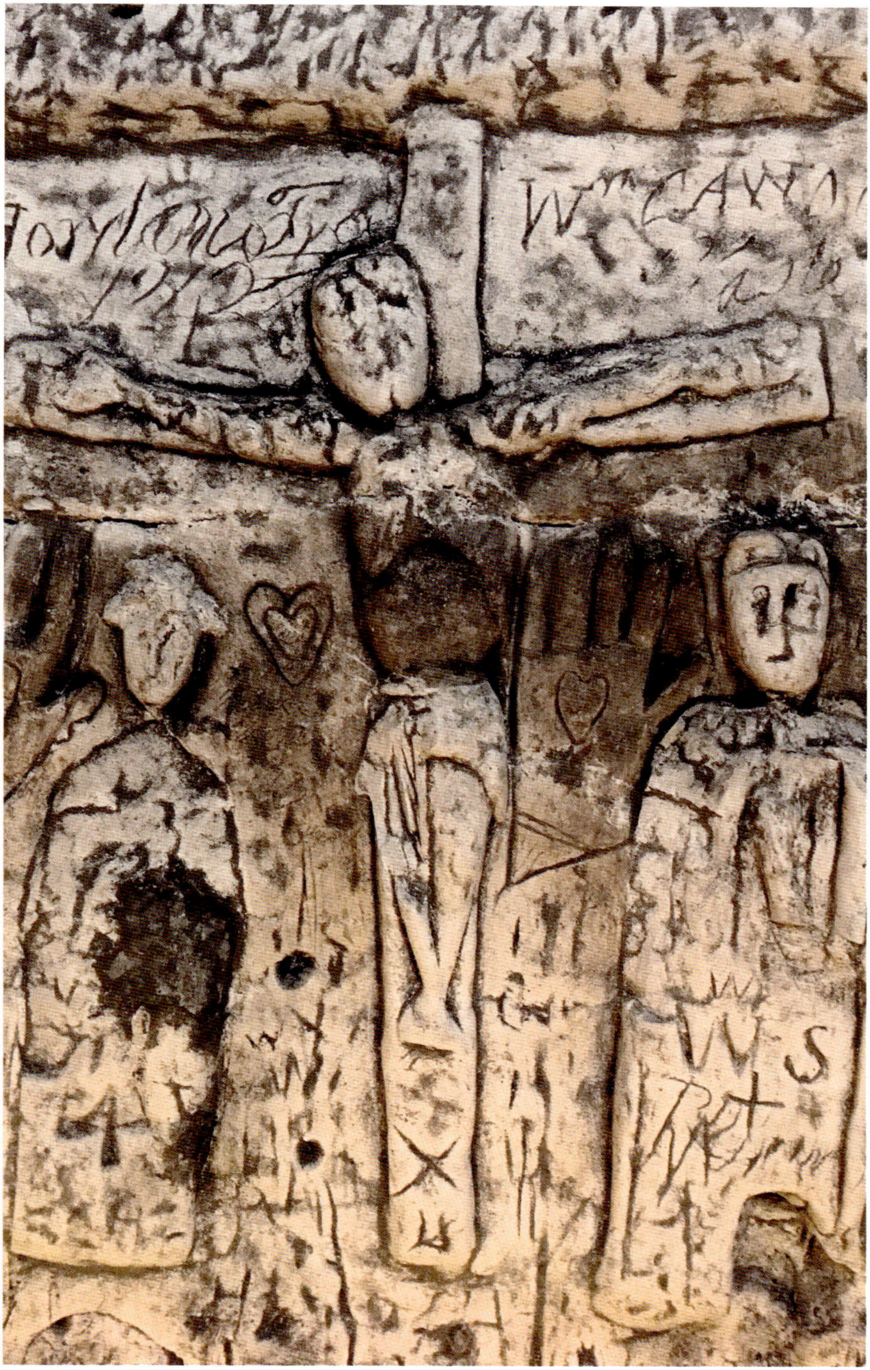

St. Mary's Church
Ashwell

St. Mary's sits at the heart of the village of Ashwell and dates from the 14th century. Its most striking feature is the tower which, at 176 feet, is the tallest in Hertfordshire. It houses six bells dating from the 18th century with the heaviest weighing nearly a ton.

The church has several outstanding features including a cross with a sculpture of *The Risen Christ* and a series of works by Percy Sheldrick, a master weaver from the William Morris workshops.

Medieval graffiti can be found throughout the building and it is recommended to study the website prior to visiting as it provides a great deal of guidance on how to interpret the messages. In recent years there has been an annual music festival each May.

Further Information

22

Mill Street, Ashwell, Baldock, SG7 5LY.

www.stmarysashwell.org.uk

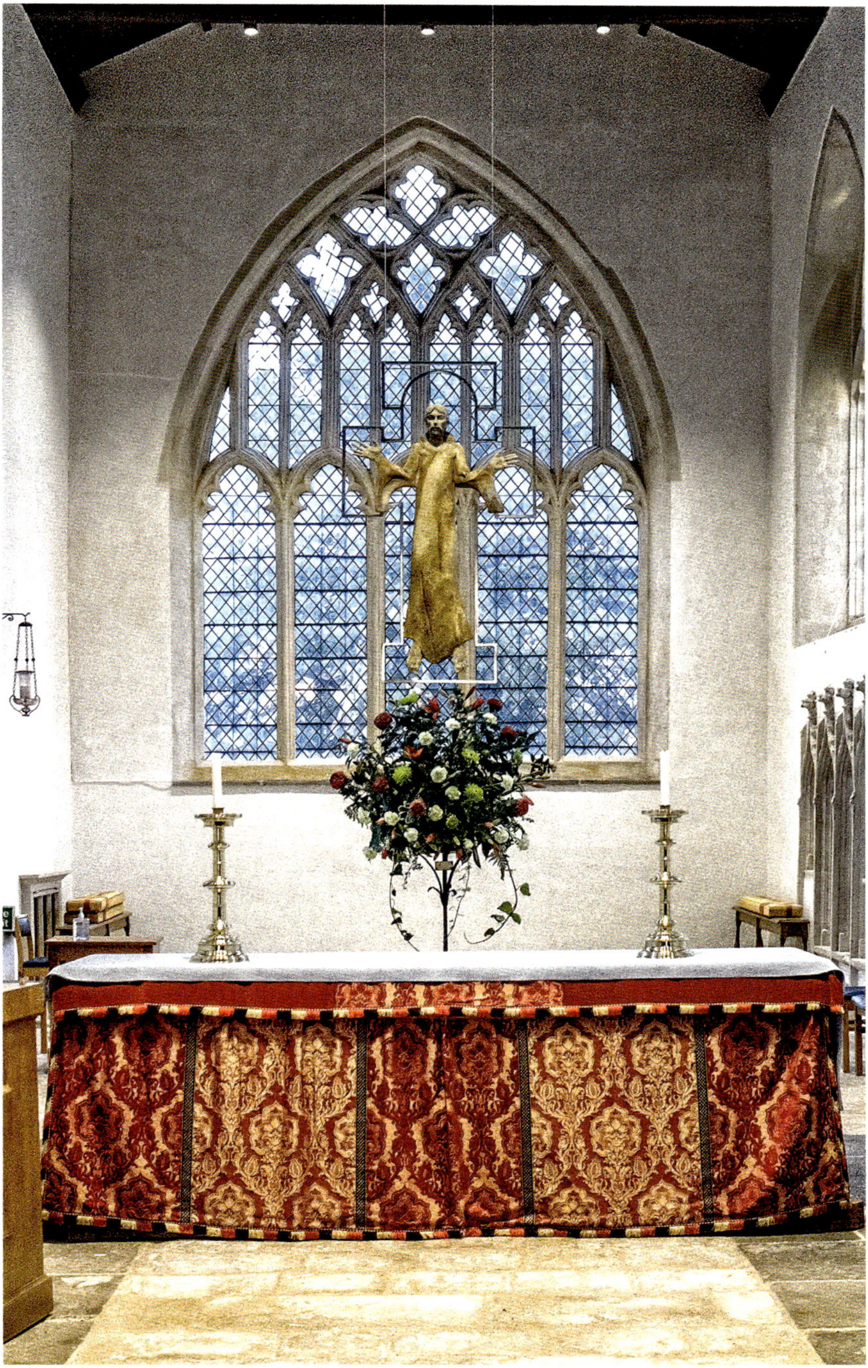

Lavender Fields
Ickleford

Lavender can be found from the Mediterranean and Middle East to India and was even identified in the tomb of Tutankhamun. Long associated with its medicinal qualities, it is believed to have been introduced into the UK by the Romans who relied on its antiseptic properties.

Fast forward to the Elizabethans who used it as both perfume and medicine. In the 1500s the small market town of Hitchin first saw the blossoming of these plants, as well as an industry, but by the 1760s Hitchin's association with lavender became firmly rooted when Harry Perks established a pharmacy.

Queen Victoria was presented with a bottle of Hitchin lavender essential oil in 1851, as was Queen Elizabeth II when she visited in 2002. These fields, containing rows of lavender stretching to the equivalent of 30 miles, offer spectacular views over rural Bedfordshire and Hertfordshire.

Further Information

23

Cadwell Farm, Ickleford, Hitchin, SG5 3UA.

www.hitchinlavender.com

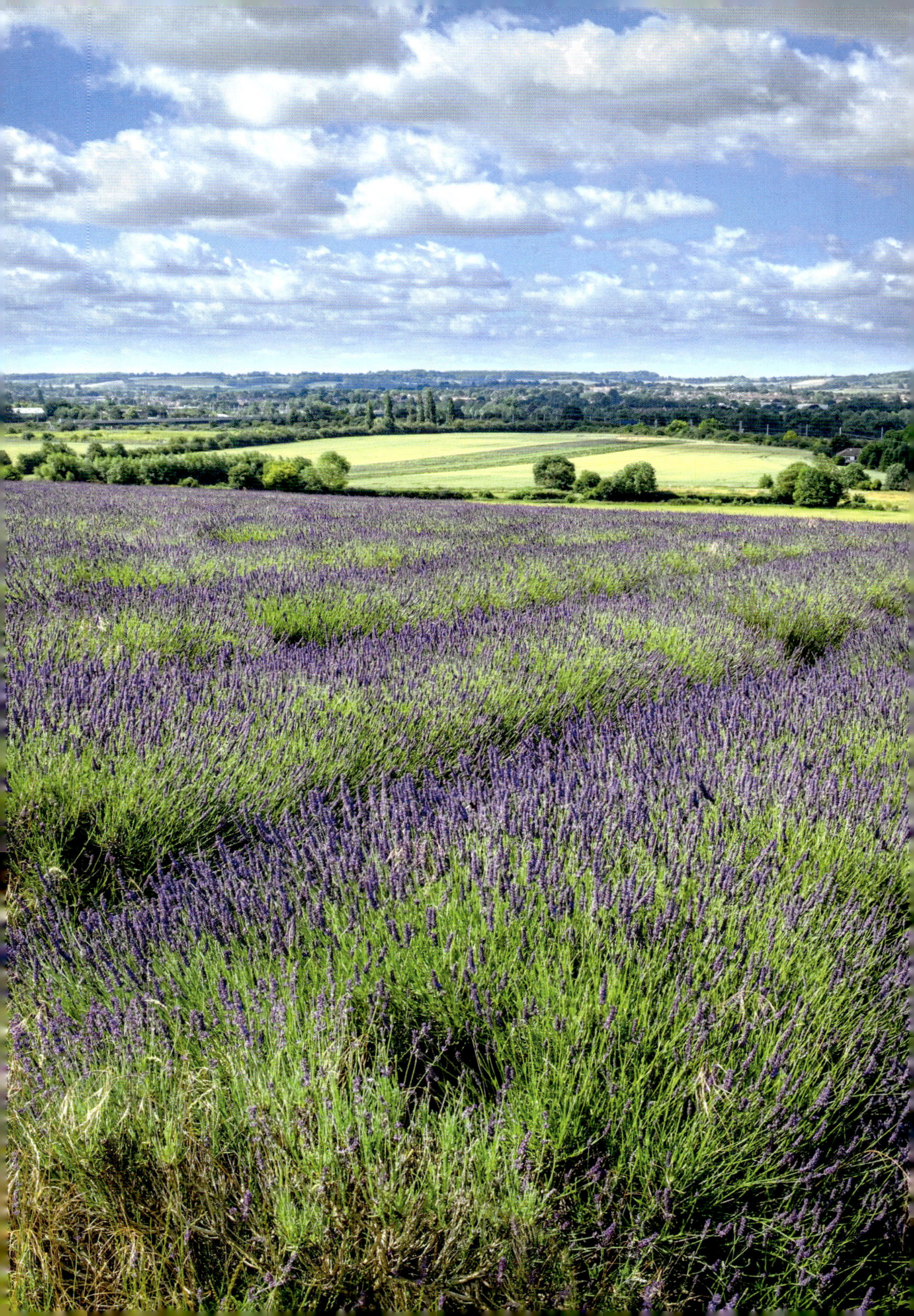

British Schools Museum
Hitchin

The beautiful market town of Hitchin boasts one of the region's hidden gems: the British Schools Museum.

The site has been a centre for curious minds for over 200 years and the Grade II listed building is an important historical example of school architecture. The infamous education reformer, Joseph Lancaster, founded schools for boys, girls and infants across the country, opening up access to education for all.

His revolutionary schoolroom design was copied the world over and the museum proudly maintains the last remaining example in the world.

Visitors today can find out about his legacy, those who benefited from his system and reminisce as they travel through 19th century classrooms. Rolling exhibitions, craft activities and a series of events will always make this gem of a place a fun day out for all the family.

Further Information

24

41/42 Queen Street, Hitchin, SG4 9TS.

www.britishschoolsmuseum.org.uk

Access: Please check website for details on activities and tours.

What's Nearby: North Herts Museum.
www.northhertsmuseum.org

Images: © Courtesy of British Schools Museum.

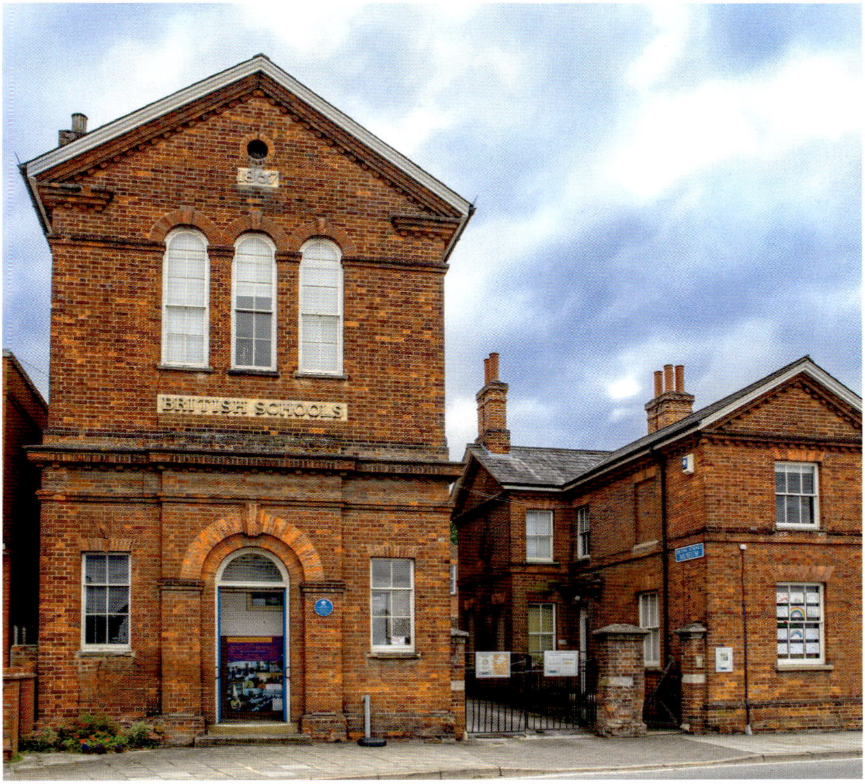
BRITISH SCHOOLS

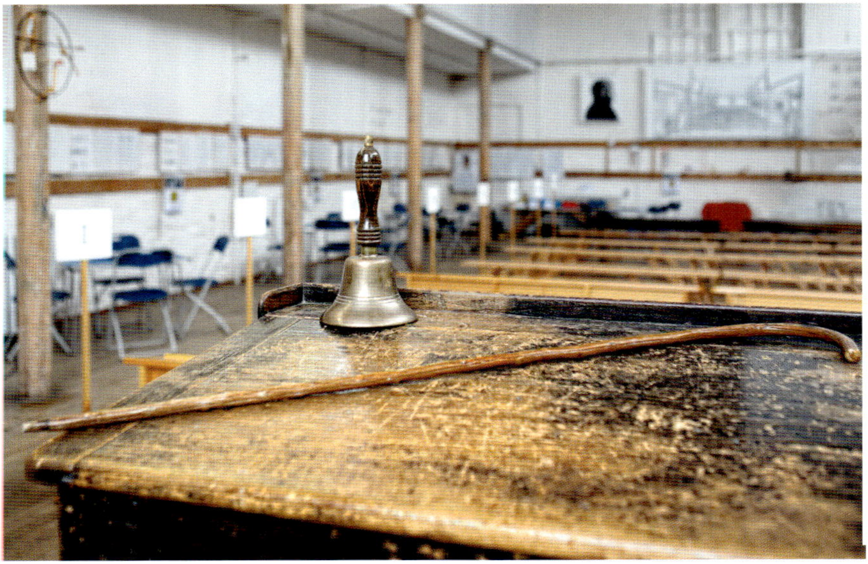

St. Paul's Walden Bury

Hitchen

This charming small stately home was the English home of Queen Elizabeth the Queen Mother until she married. Her brother's descendants now live here.

The remarkable Grade 1 listed garden covers over 50 acres, laid out about 1720 when the house was built. It retains the original formal design based on the classical patte d'oie (goose foot) architecture. It was in this garden that the then Duke of York proposed and was finally accepted.

Visitors can explore long avenues of clipped beech hedges stretching out into the Hertfordshire countryside and discover temples and statues which appear unexpectedly as vistas open up.

The woodland garden is notable for its wildflowers, rhododendrons and magnolias, many of which were sourced in the Himalayas and planted over the last 80 years.

Further Information

25

St. Paul's Walden, Hitchin, SG4 8BP.

www.stpaulswaldenbury.co.uk

Images: © Courtesy of Marianne Majerus/St Paul's Walden Bury.

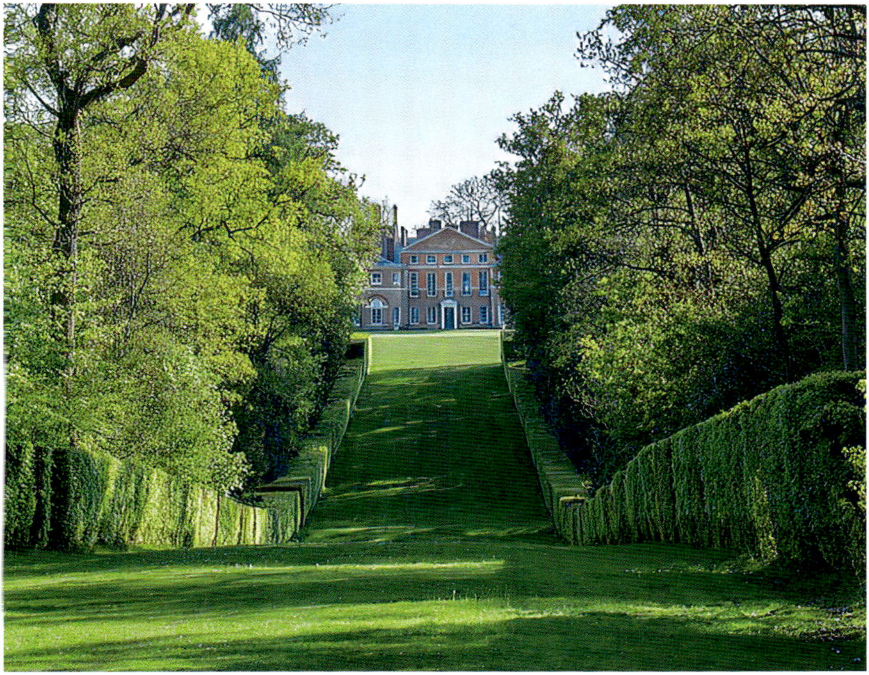

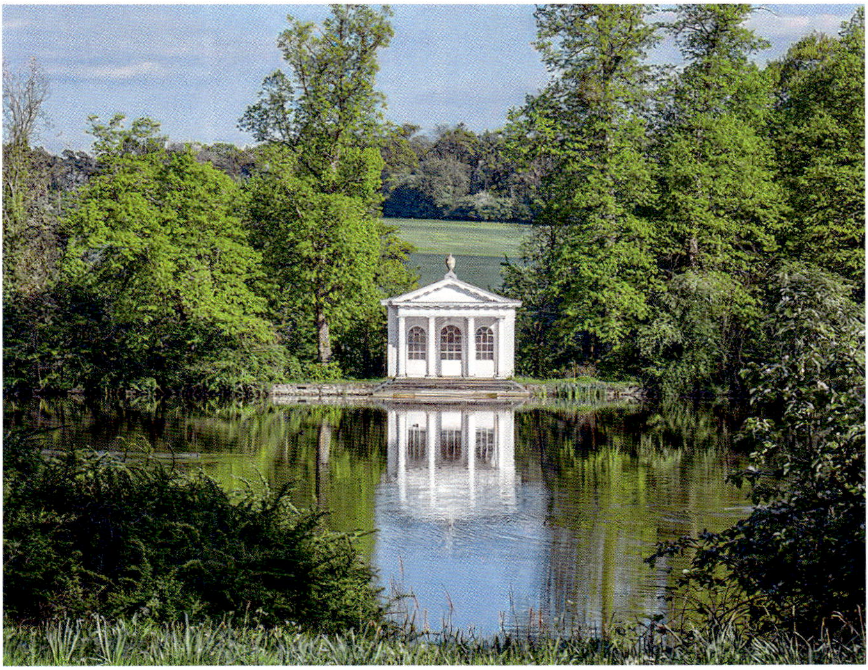

Knebworth House

Knebworth

The Victorian exterior of Knebworth House belies its long history dating back to Tudor times. Set in 250 acres of beautiful rolling Hertfordshire countryside with 28 acres of formal gardens, it has been in the Lytton family for over 19 generations. A visit offers an extraordinary walk through 500 years of history.

Stories and heirlooms reflect the family's contribution to literature, politics and foreign service. Visits from people as diverse as Charles Dickens, Winston Churchill and Queen Elizabeth I have also added to Knebworth's rich heritage.

Highlights of the gardens include the lawns and avenues of lime trees designed by Sir Edward Lutyens and the herb garden recreated from Gertrude Jekyll's original design. The historic parkland, home to red and sika deer, is the perfect location for walks and picnics.

Further Information

26

Knebworth House, Gardens & Park, Knebworth, SG1 2AX.

www.knebworthhouse.com

Access: Entry fee required for house and garden access. Please check website for up to date opening times.

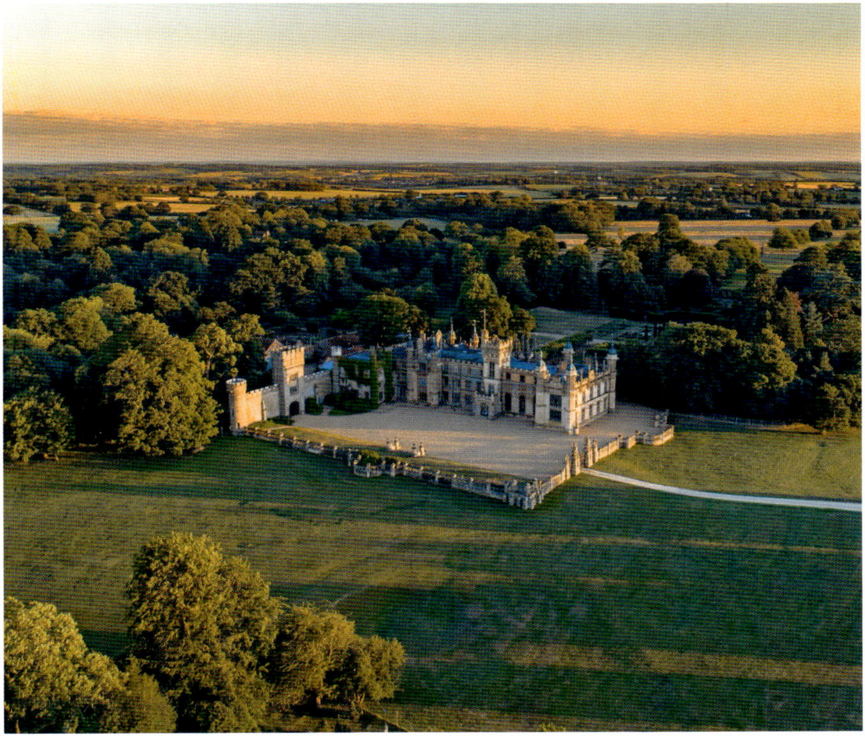

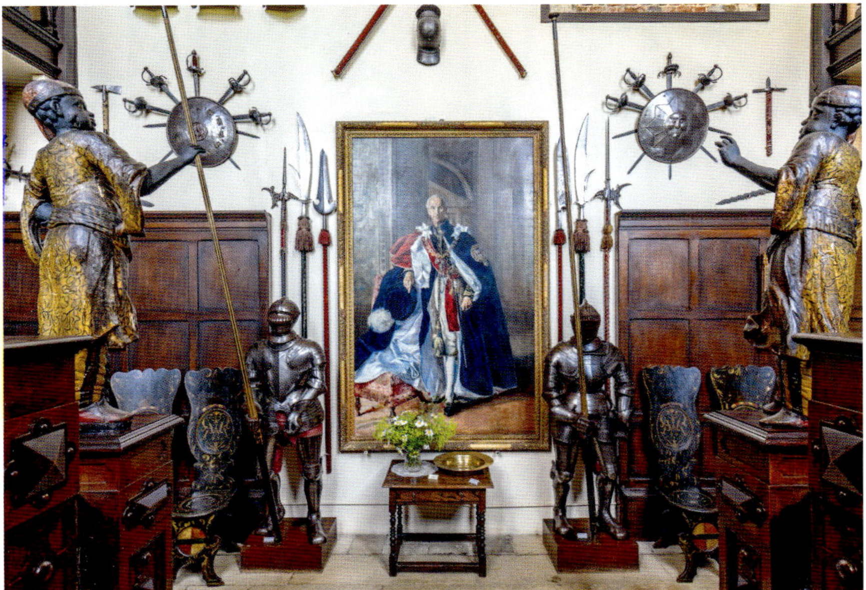

Benington Lordship Garden
Benington

Situated in the ancient village of Benington, the gardens at Benington Lordship have been attracting visitors since the 1920s. The gardens are informally arranged around the ruin of a Norman motte and bailey castle, demolished by King John around 1213, which is thought to be the only surviving example of vernacular Norman stonework in Hertfordshire.

More visible is the dramatic Pulham folly, completed in 1838, consisting of two magnificent neo Norman towers and a curtain wall. The house, built circa 1700 with the addition of an Edwardian wing, offers spectacular views over surrounding parkland. The seasonal gardens have much to offer, ranging from the famous snowdrop displays in February to the full summer glory of a double herbaceous border and the more structured formality of the rose and walled gardens.

Further Information

27

Benington, Nr Stevenage, SG2 7BS.

www.beningtonlordship.co.uk
www.beningtonlordship.co.uk/snowdrops

Benington Motte and Bailey Castle.
www.historicengland.org.uk/listing/the-list/list-entry/1007844

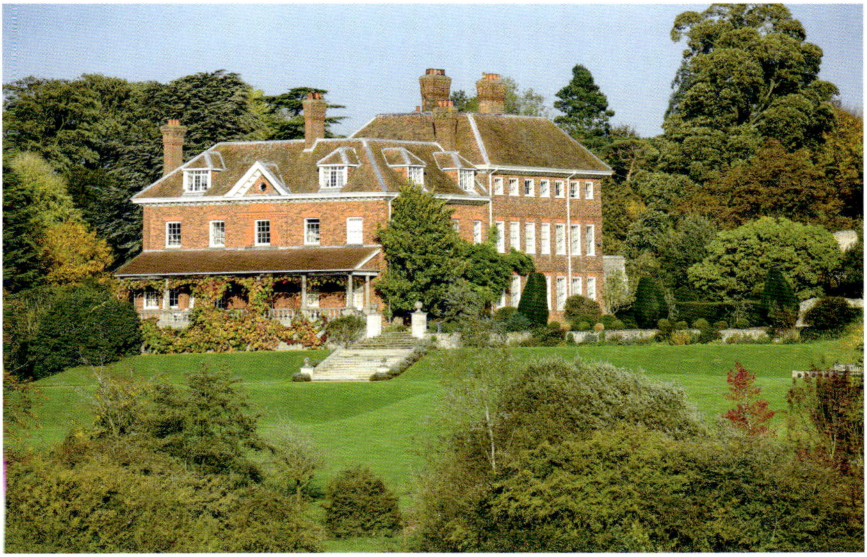

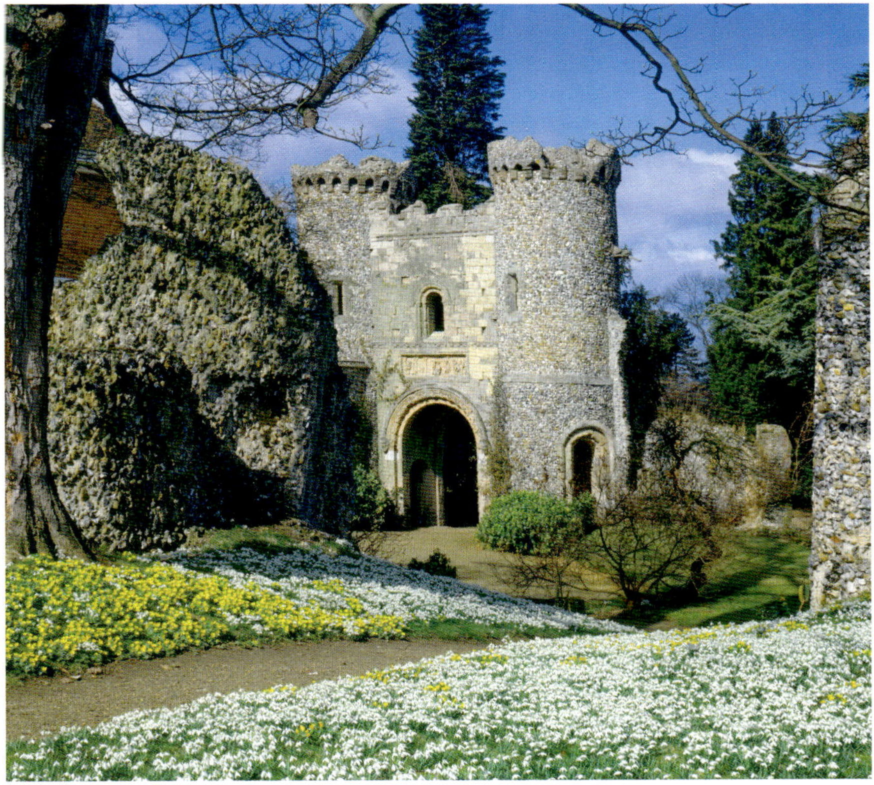

Forge Museum
Much Hadham

The forge is set within a Grade II listed building which dates to the 15th century in the picturesque village of Much Hadham. It retains unique Tudor wall paintings which reveal details of Tudor fashion and the increasing social status of the Hertfordshire Newce family.

The forge and bellows were added as part of a 17th century barn conversion which subsequently gained a shoeing room and blacksmith's shop. There is a resident blacksmith who runs events and experience days independently of the museum.

St. Andrew's Church nearby is worth a visit as it features the only stained-glass window designed by Henry Moore.

Further Information

28

High Street, Much Hadham, SG10 6BS.

www.hadhammuseum.org.uk
www.muchhadhamforge.co.uk (blacksmith)

Access: Entry is free, but a guided walk through Much Hadham can be booked at a modest cost and includes a visit to St. Andrew's Church.

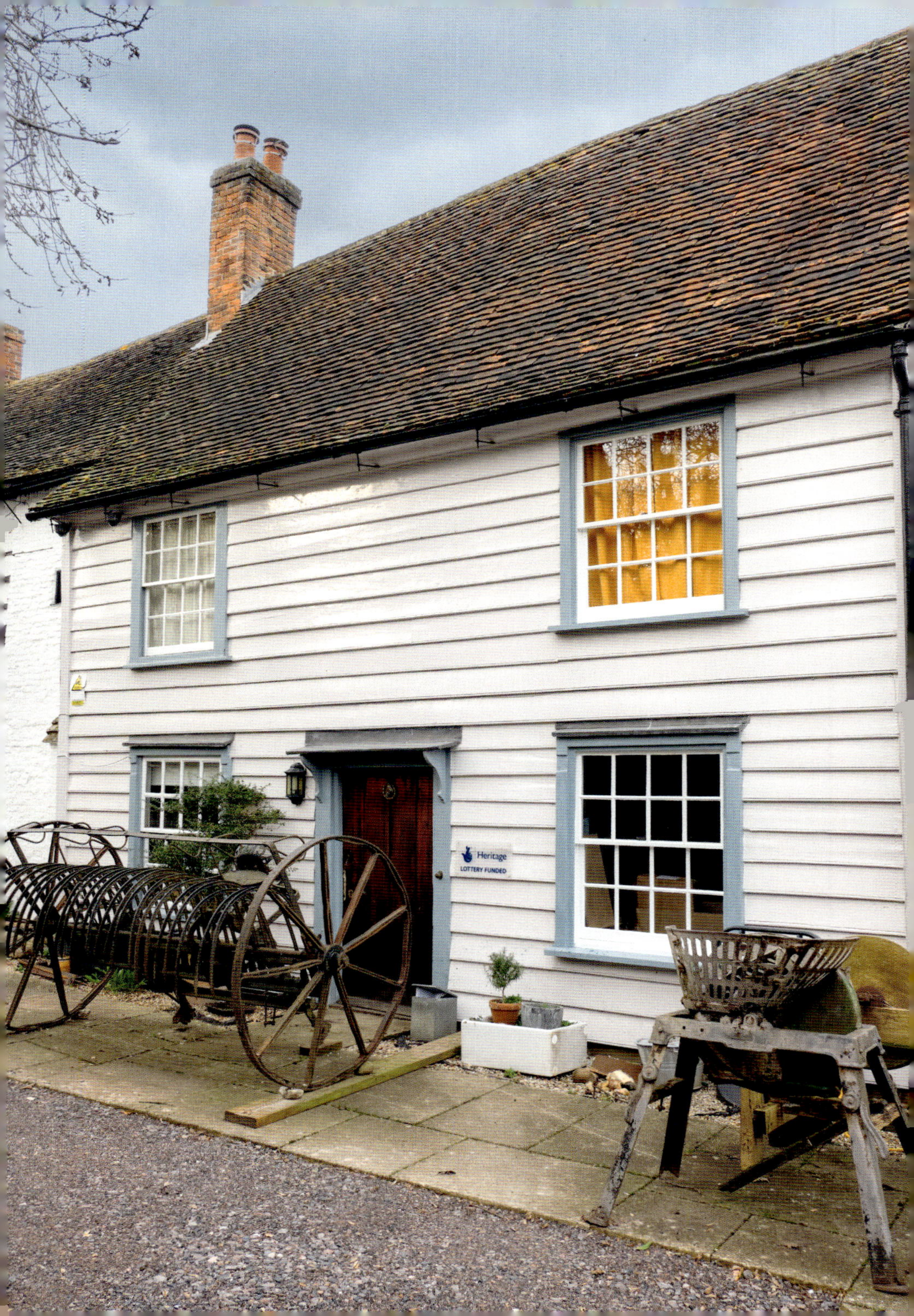
Heritage
LOTTERY FUNDED

Henry Moore Studios and Gardens
Much Hadham

Henry Moore lived at Perry Green for 40 years and it is here that he created some of his greatest work. Today, his studios and gardens are a highly regarded visitor destination with over 70 acres of grounds to explore and view the artist's iconic work against the landscape in which they were conceived. It is also the home of the Henry Moore Foundation, created in 1977 to encourage public appreciation of the visual arts.

Moore's old studios are open to the public, showing his creative process from small maquettes through to monumental outdoor sculptures. His former home Hoglands gives a touching insight into Moore's domestic life, including his remarkable book collection and a Picasso painting which he kept in his kitchen. A rotating exhibition programme showcases Moore's textiles, tapestries and drawings.

Further Information

29

Dane Tree House, Perry Green, Much Hadham, SG10 6EE.

www.henry-moore.org

Access: Admission fees apply. Group bookings and tours available. Please check website for opening times.

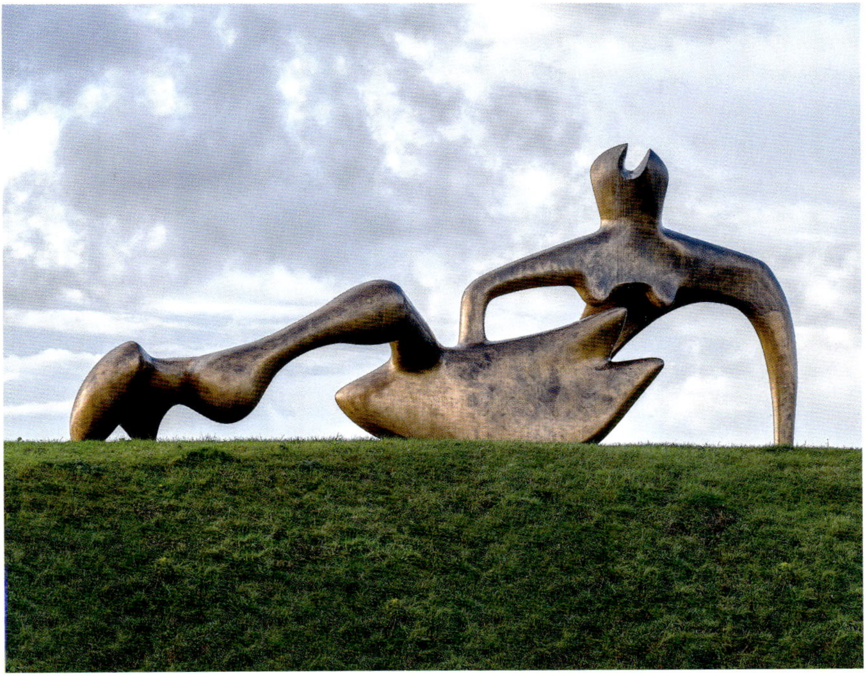

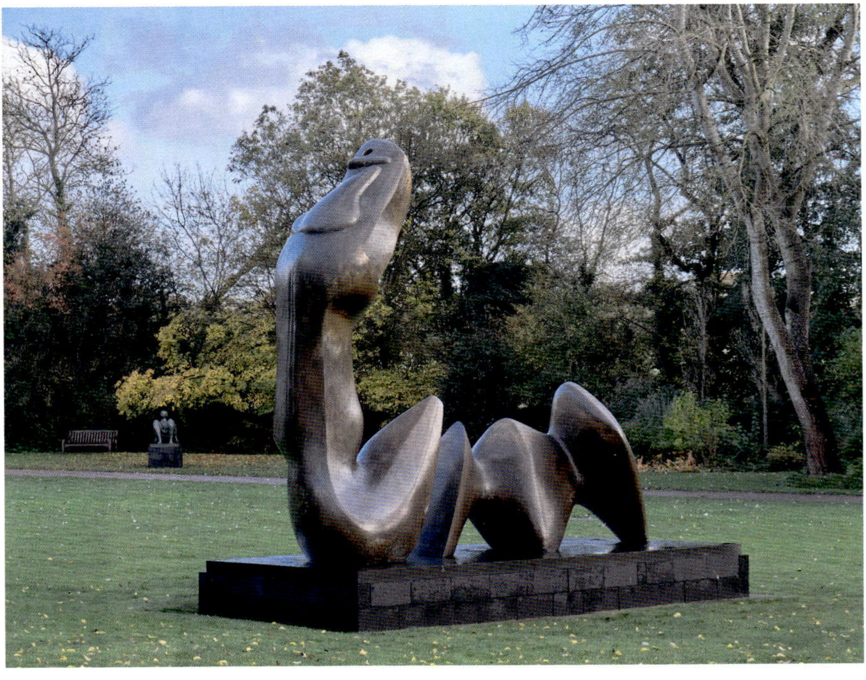

Roman Baths
Welwyn

Visitors can no longer take a hot bath - the boiler went out 1,800 years ago when the Romans left!

They can, however, see fascinating remains and learn how the Romans liked to relax with an elegant culture of bathing and admire their creativity and style. The bath house remains were once part of a fine villa. The layout of the cold, warm and hot rooms and the heating system are remarkably well preserved. The baths are ingeniously preserved in a steel vault in a most surprising location, under the A1(M) motorway at its junction with the A1000 – just off the central roundabout of the Welwyn By-Pass.

Additional displays include archaeological finds from the Welwyn area and an exhibition devoted to the history of the site, which was uncovered during the 1960s and 70s.

Further Information

30

Welwyn By-Pass Road, Welwyn , AL6 9FG.

www.welhat.gov.uk/romanbaths

Access: Car parking and facilities on site. Activities, premises and exhibitions accessible to all.

What's Nearby: Danesbury Fernery, developed in 1860 and "the best to be found in the Home Counties" www.danesburyfernery.org.uk

Image: © Courtesy of Welwyn Hatfield District Council.

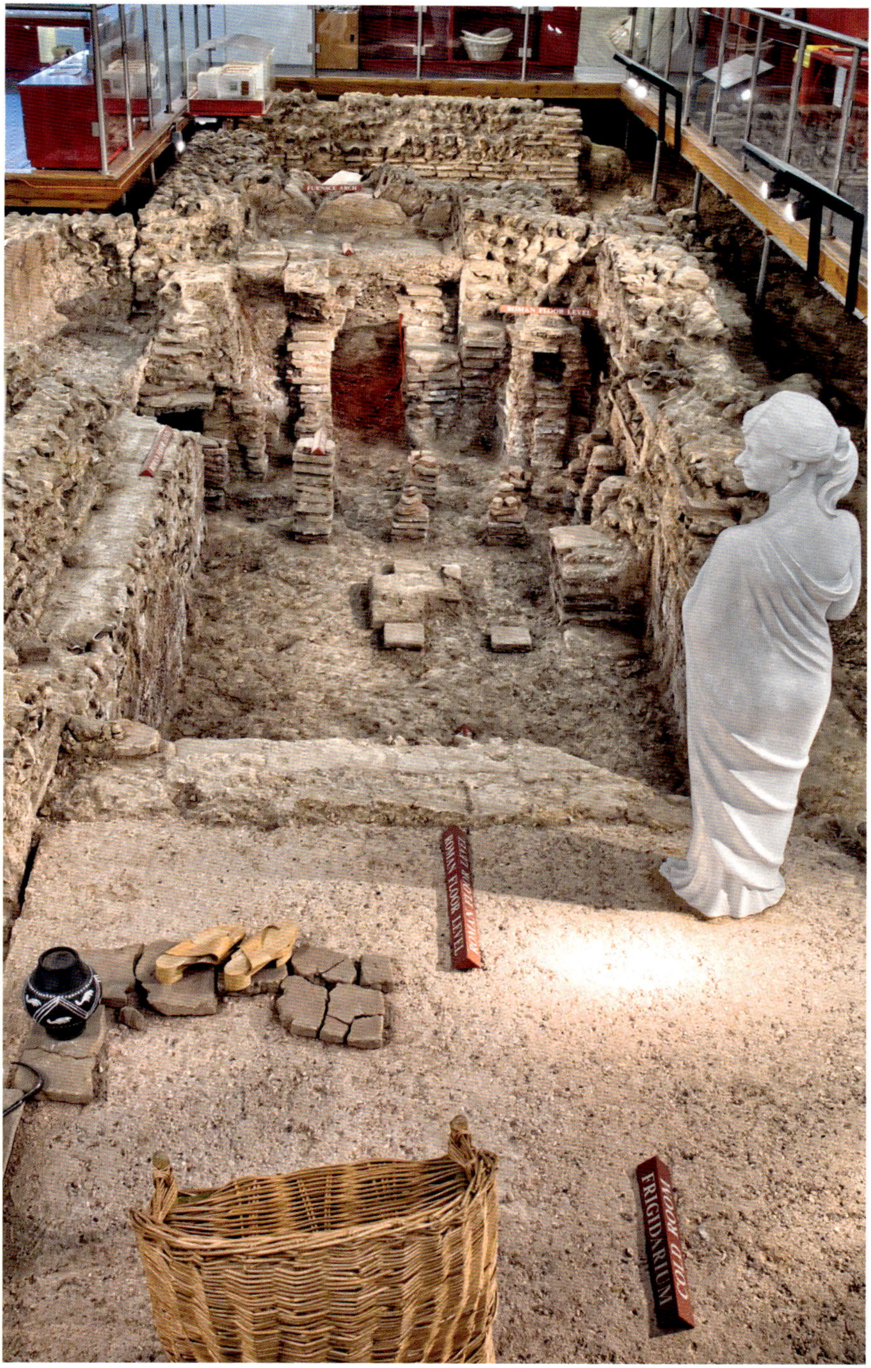
ROMAN FLOOR LEVEL
FRIGIDARIUM

St. Michael and All Angels
Waterford

This church was built in 1871, financed by the Smith family and designed by the architect Henry Woodyer in the Victorian Gothic style. Its interior contains a treasure trove of Pre-Raphaelite delights including stained glass windows by William Morris, Edward Burne-Jones and Ford Madox Brown. The *Miriam* window has been described as one of the best examples of Victorian glass anywhere. There are wall and floor mosaics by Powells of Whitefriars and the reredos displays saints and angels set behind a marble arcade.

A second generation of artists added works during the 20th century, in particular, a striking stained glass of St. Cecilia by Karl Parsons.

Further Information

31

High Road, Waterford, SG14 2PS.

www.explorechurches.org/church/st-michael-all-angels-waterford

Access: Generally open to visitors. There is a Facebook page that displays helpful information.

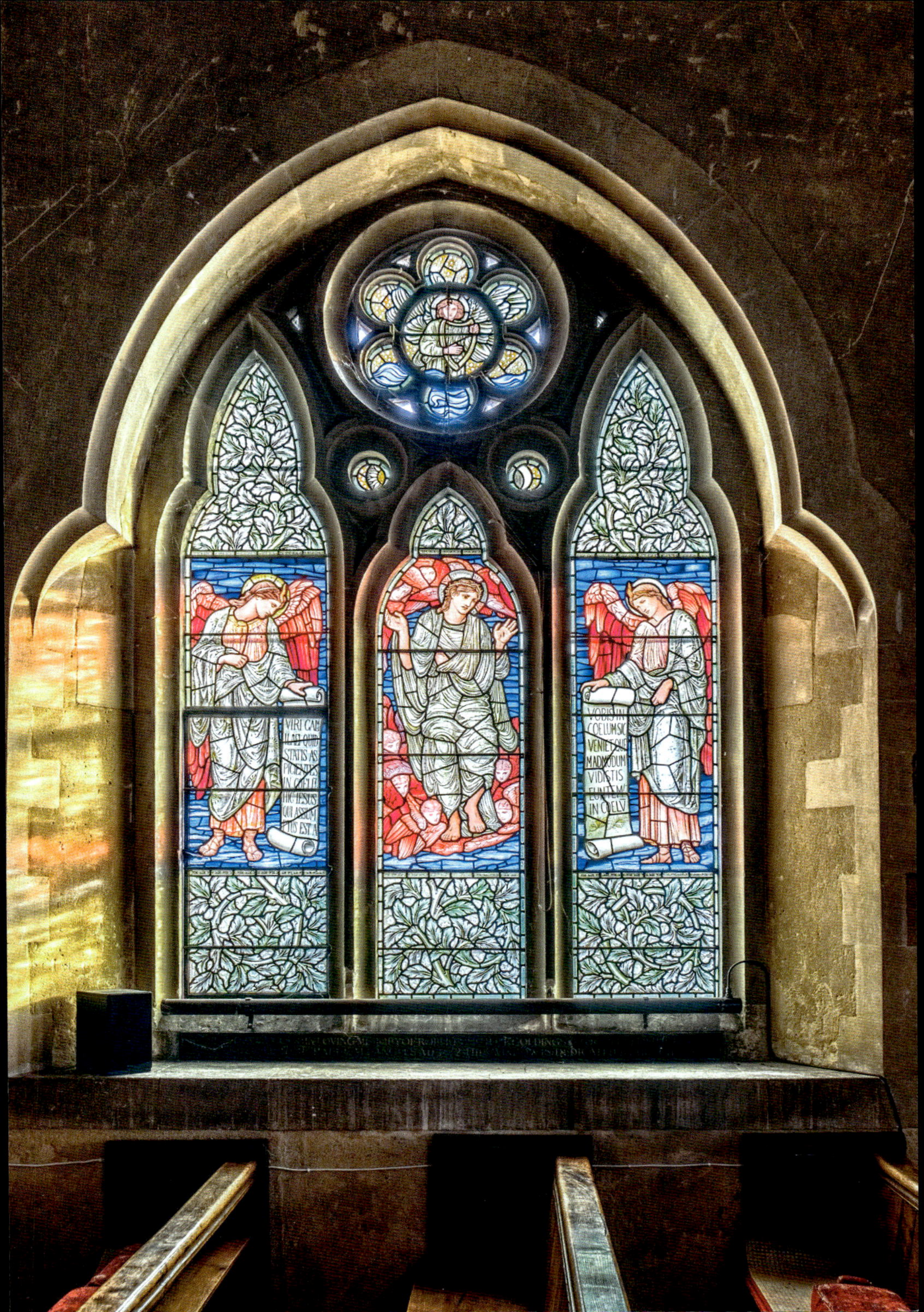
VIRI GAL
STATIS AS
HIC IESUS
VOBIS IN
COELUM SIC
MADMODUM
VIDISTIS
IN COELV

Friends Meeting House
Hertford

The Religious Society of Friends was founded in the mid-17th century by, amongst others, George Fox, who rejected the idea that the faithful needed intermediaries to the divine. Fox reputedly told one judge that the only authority he trembled before was God, leading the judge to scornfully dismiss him as a "quaker" – a name which stuck.

Against this backdrop, the construction of the Hertford Meeting House was completed in 1670 at a cost of £243.6s with donations in money, land, building materials and labour from Quakers in the proximity. George Fox visited at least three times.

The simple design of this Grade 1 listed building aims to give Quakers the freedom to worship in their own way, all equal before God. Worldwide, it is their oldest purpose-built venue to remain in uninterrupted use and 2020 marked its 350th anniversary.

Further Information

32

50 Railway Street, Hertford, SG14 1BA.

www.hertfordandhitchinquakers.org.uk/hertford

Access: Visitors are welcome on open days - details of which are listed on the website.

Image: © Courtesy of Ian Burgess.

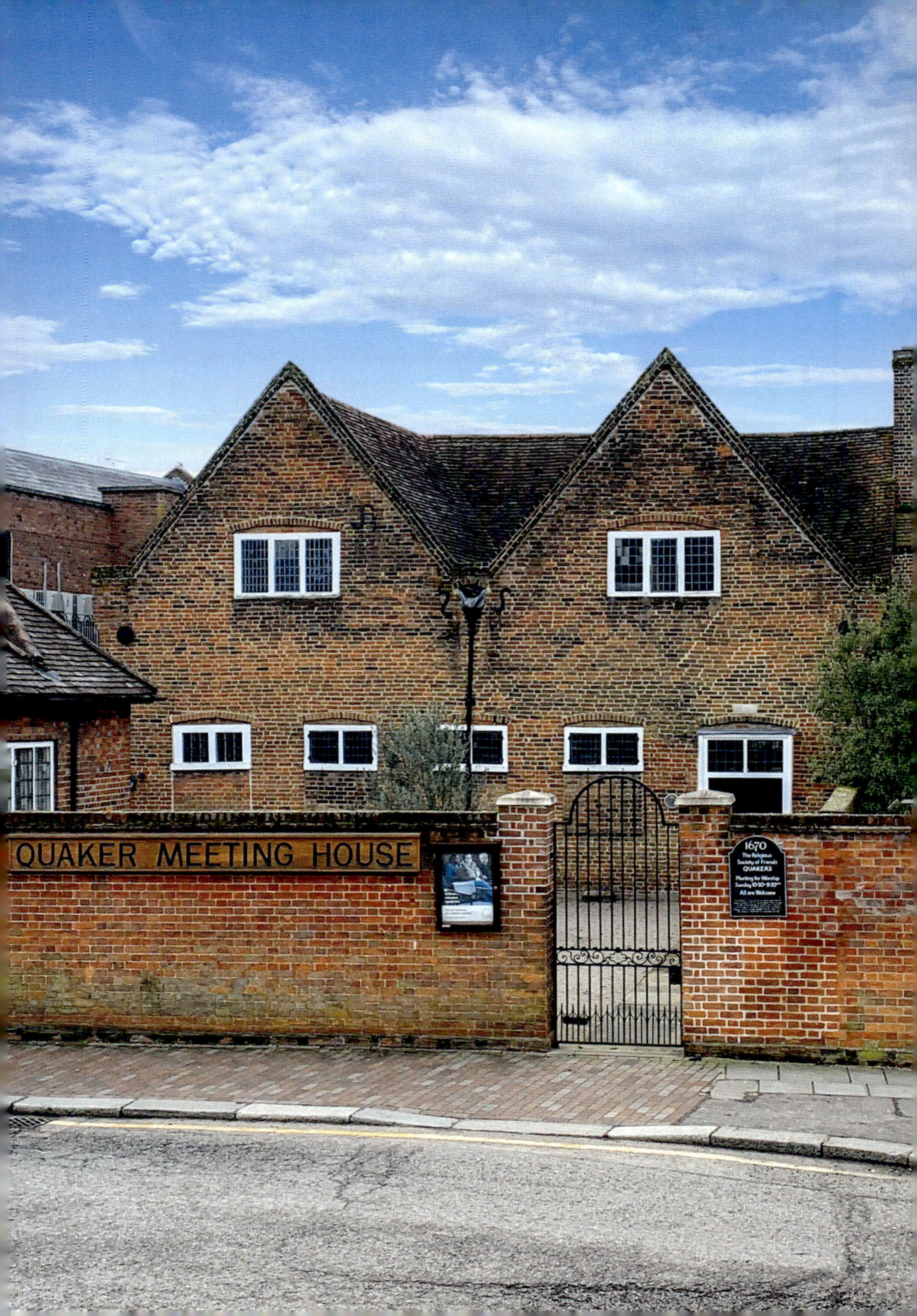
QUAKER MEETING HOUSE
1670
The Religious
Society of Friends
QUAKERS
Meeting for Worship
All are Welcome

Scott's Grotto

Ware

The poet John Scott moved from London to Hertfordshire in the middle of the 18th century seeking cleaner air. He set about a series of projects for the house and gardens which included the fashion for building grottoes. This consisted of a series of interconnected chambers extending 67 feet into the chalk hillside. The chambers and tunnels are lined with shells, flints and pieces of coloured glass. Sadly, as the property passed through ownership, the Grotto fell into disrepair.

In the 1980s the Ware Society began the significant enterprise of renovation, supported by the local authority and English Heritage.

Entry is limited to certain days so it is recommended to check the website before visiting.

Further Information

33

34 Scotts Road, Ware, SG12 9JG.

www.scotts-grotto.org

What's Nearby: Gazebos of Ware, River Lee.
www.waretourism.org.uk
Rye House.
www.hertsmemories.org.uk/content/herts-history/places/historic-houses/rye_house

Images: © Courtesy of Scott's Grotto.

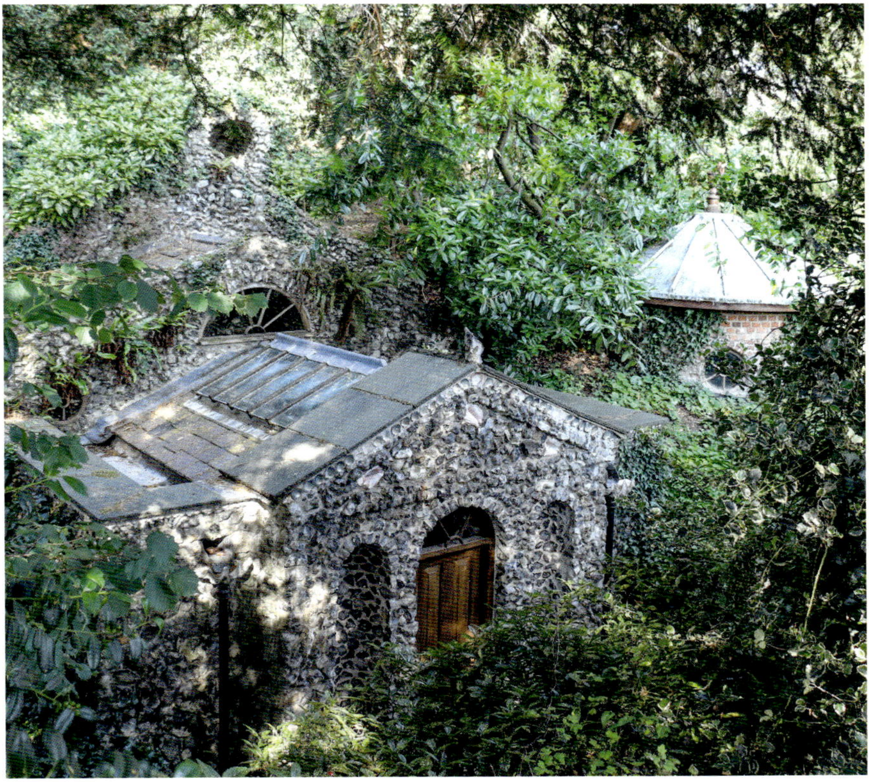

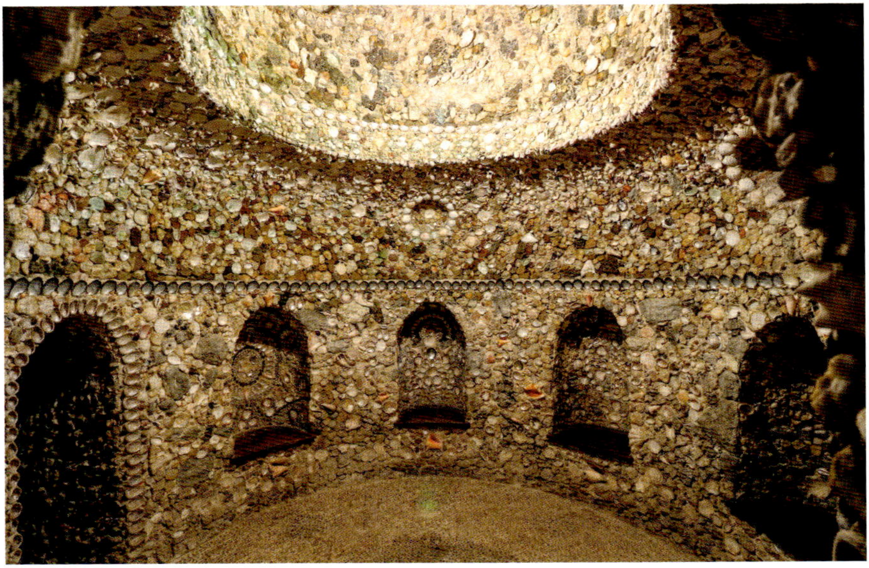

Mill Green Museum and Mill

Hatfield

There has been a mill recorded at Mill Green since the Domesday Book of 1086, where it is listed as being owned by the Bishops of Ely at 'Hetfelle'. Today that tradition of almost 1,000 years of milling continues, drawing on the power of the River Lea, the longest river in Hertfordshire.

The current mill was built in the 1760s and restored in 1979. It re-opened in 1986 as a working mill and museum, since when it's been teaching visitors about the science behind the loaf of bread they eat. Visitors can see the historic water mill in action as it produces stoneground wholemeal flour, which is available to buy in the shop.

A knot garden has been created and the riverside setting is ideal for picnics. A variety of themed days are on offer which are popular with families.

Further Information

34

Mill Bush Hall Lane, Mill Green, Hatfield, AL9 5PD.

www.millgreenmuseum.co.uk

Access: Entry to grounds is free with a small charge for access to the mill which is open 3 days a week. Car park and some disabled access - please check website for full details.

Image: © Courtesy of Welwyn Hatfield District Council.

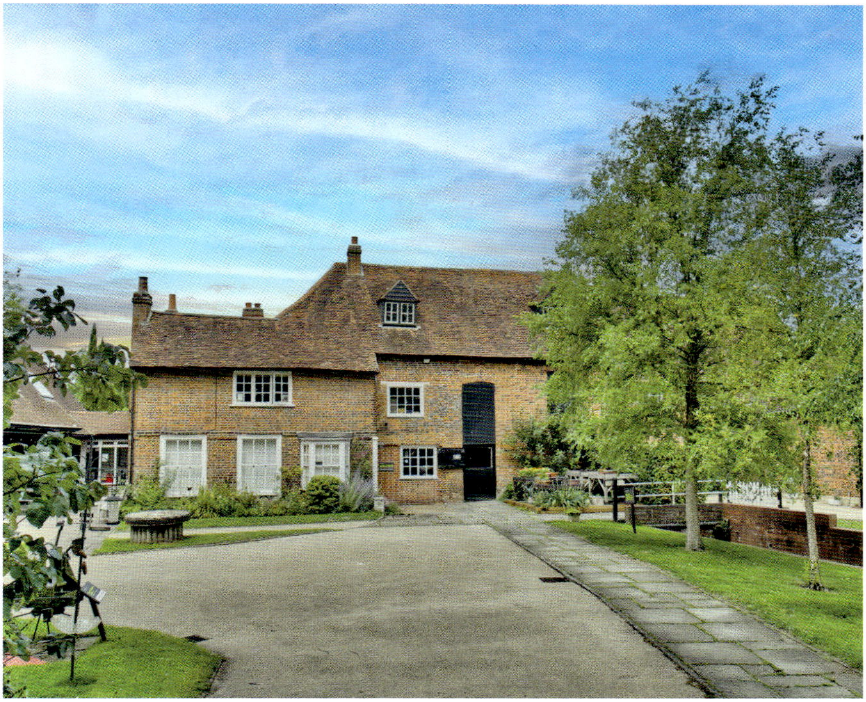

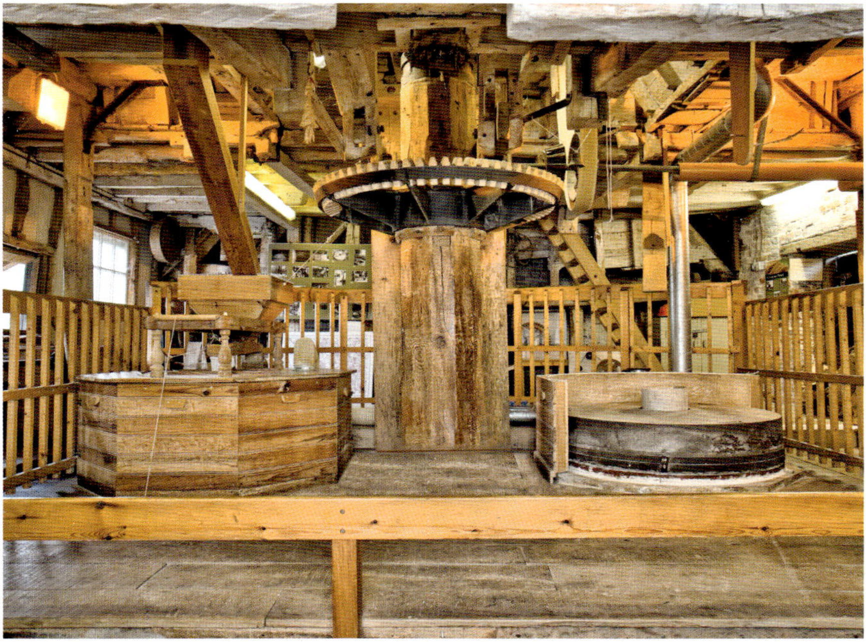

Hatfield House

Hatfield

Hatfield House has its place in history as the residence of Queen Elizabeth I when she learned of her ascension to the English throne. The current house was built on the site of a former royal palace in the Jacobean style in 1611 by Robert Cecil, Chief Minister to King James I. It remains in the ownership of the Cecil family. It abounds with references to these two monarchs, including the famous *Rainbow Portrait* of Elizabeth and treasures collected over the last 400 years. Rooms such as the King James Drawing Room are steeped in history.

Hatfield Park and Gardens bring their own pleasures, including the box-bordered Old Palace Garden and the Sundial Garden. The parklands provide woodland walks of various lengths.

Further Information

35

Hatfield Park, Hatfield, AL9 5HX.

www.hatfield-house.co.uk

Access: Throughout the year Hatfield House has a varied programme of exhibitions and events. Entrance fees apply and seasonal opening times are detailed on the website.

What's Nearby: Hatfield Old Town. www.hatfieldhistory.uk/history

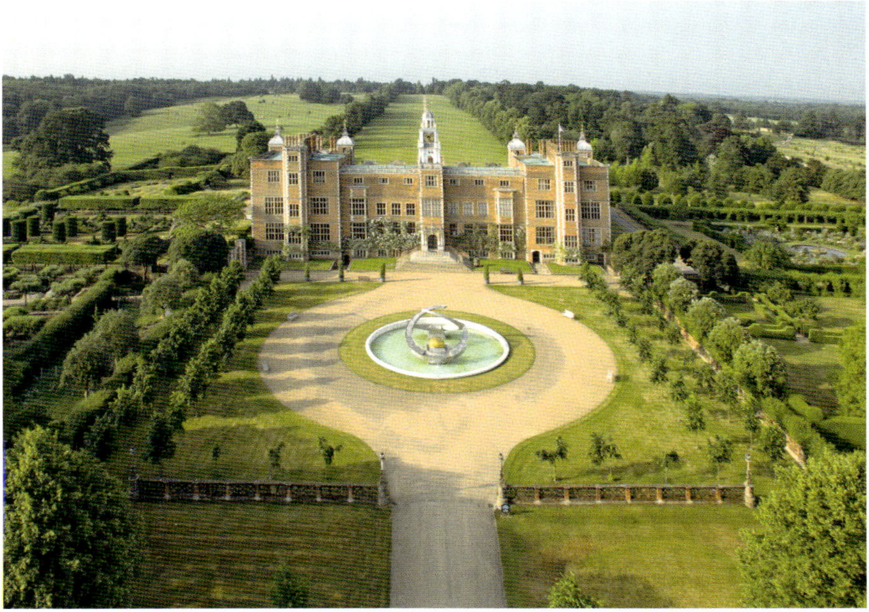

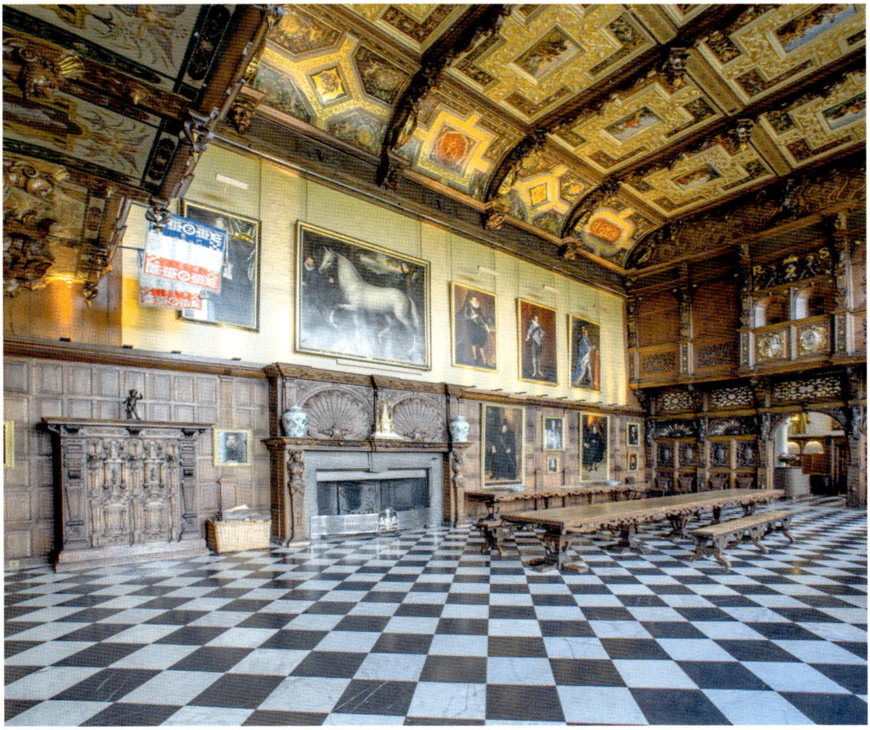

Shaw's Corner
Ayot St. Lawrence

Built as the new rectory for the village in 1902, Shaw's Corner is an Edwardian Arts & Crafts influenced house which, from 1906, became the country residence of renowned Irish playwright George Bernard Shaw.

Initially renting the house, Shaw and his wife, Charlotte Payne-Townshend, eventually bought it in 1920. After purchasing additional land from his friend, the Antarctic explorer Apsley Cherry-Garrard*, the garden was extended to include woodland around the more formal beds. Left to the National Trust by Shaw on his death in 1950, visitors can enjoy interiors, art collections and artefacts arranged much as he left them and which give an insight to his strong views on socialism, feminism and pacificism.

The peaceful, attractive gardens contain the gem of Shaw's rotating summerhouse which he used as a writing hut.

Further Information

36

Ayot St Lawrence, Nr Welwyn, AL6 9BX.

www.nationaltrust.org.uk/shaws-corner

Access: National Trust property with variety of events, exhibitions and activities throughout the year. Tours also available - please contact before visiting.

*See the entry for St. Helen's Church, Wheathampstead - Treasure no. 37.

What's Nearby: Palladian Church
www.ayotstlawrence.com

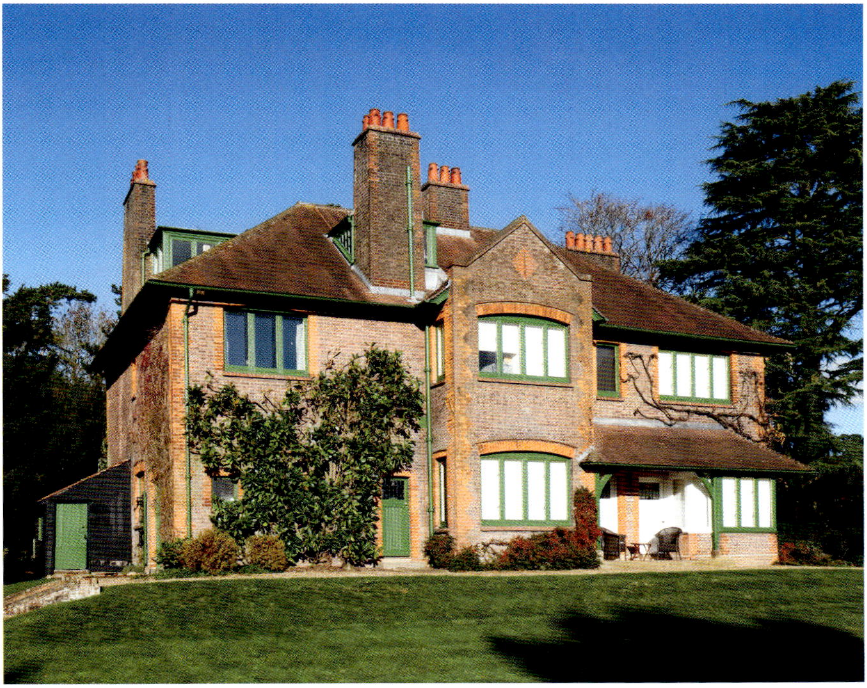

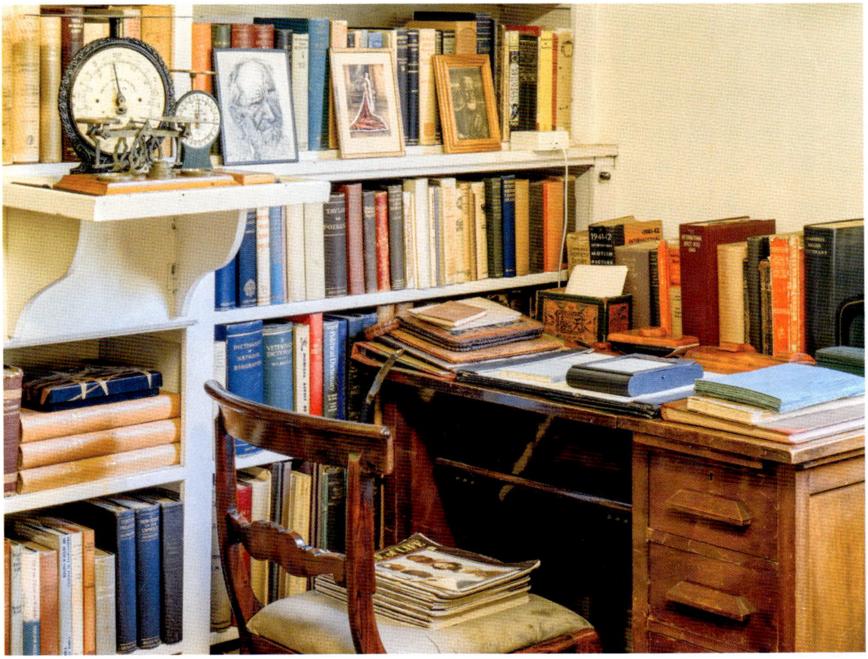

St. Helen's Church

Wheathampstead

This delightful church originates from the 13th century when the Normans replaced the wooden Saxon church on the same site, although remnants remain.

The tower's eight bell set is still used regularly. The mediaeval style spire is clad with lead arranged in a herringbone pattern. In the churchyard is the grave of Apsley George Benet Cherry-Garrard who was a member of Scott's ill-fated second Antarctic expedition and recounted his experience in his book *The Worst Journey in the World*.

A statue of Cherry-Garrard is located in the Garrard Chapel which also houses a magnificently carved reredos. Found walled up in 1865, it was restored to reveal all the artistry of its itinerant medieval stonemason, who did not quite finish his work.

Other delightful features include the Victorian restored ceiling in the chancel and the tiny 'lepers' window'.

Further Information

37

High Street, Wheathampstead, St. Albans, AL4 8AA.

www.sth-stp.org

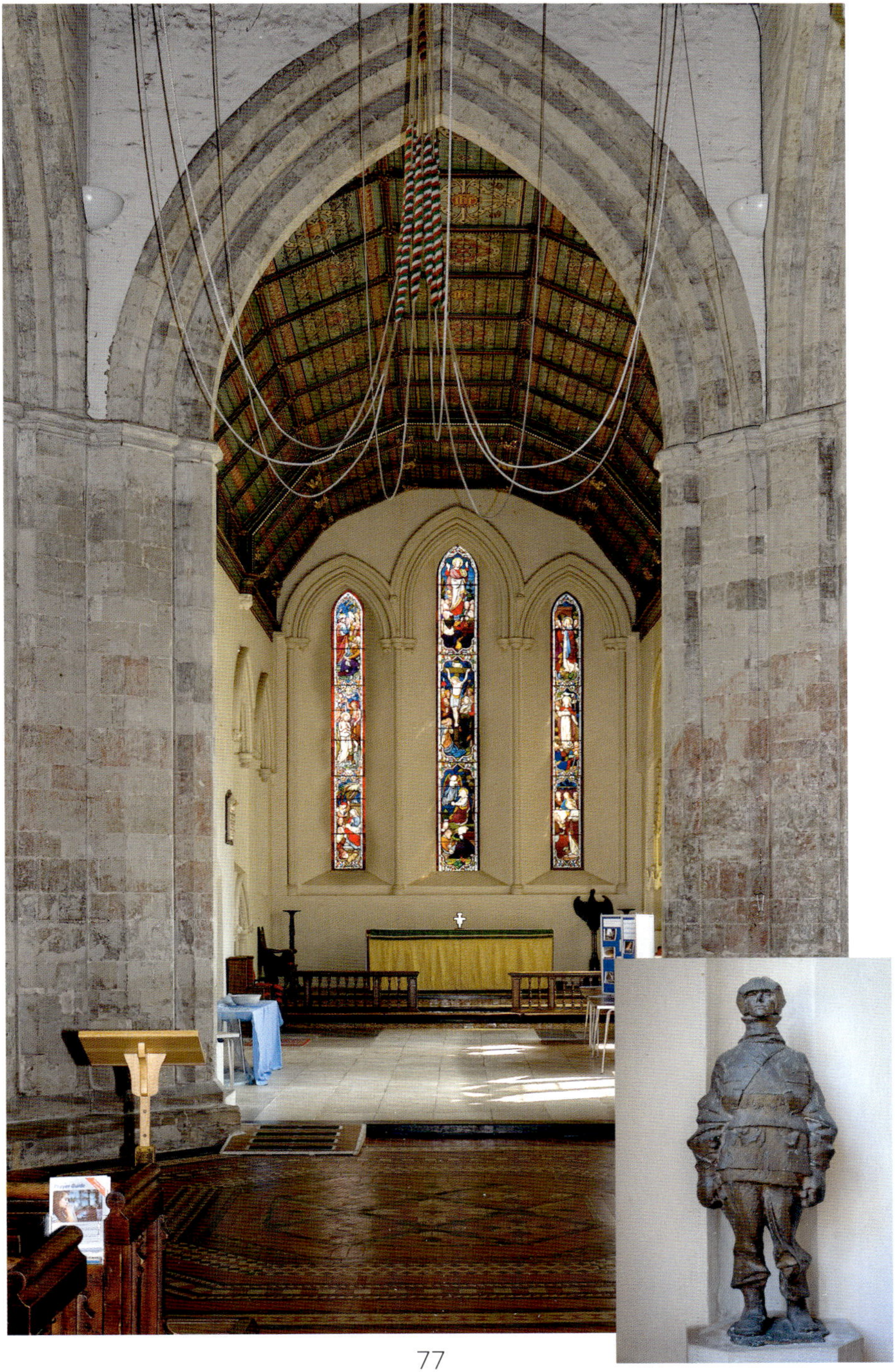

Wheathampstead Village

This pretty village, featuring many historic buildings, lies just a few miles north of St. Albans and is one of the most picturesque in Hertfordshire.

The former walled garden of the old rectory is adjacent to St. Helen's Church and is enclosed by a 19th century 'crinkle-crankle' wall. The undulating shape of these walls enabled them to be built high using only a two-brick width.

Nearby is the restored platform of the Great Northern Railway station, opened in 1860 and closed in 1967. A statue honours playwright George Bernard Shaw who often cycled to the station from his nearby home in Ayot St. Lawrence.

A prehistoric defensive ditch, The Devil's Dyke, lies to the east of the village. This is believed to be part of the remains of the ancient capital of the Celtic tribe, the Catuvellauni.

Further Information

38

On the B651, Wheathampstead, AL4 8BB.

www.wheathampsteadheritage.org.uk

What's Nearby: Shaw's Corner - see Treasure 36.
St. Helen's Church - see Treasure 37.

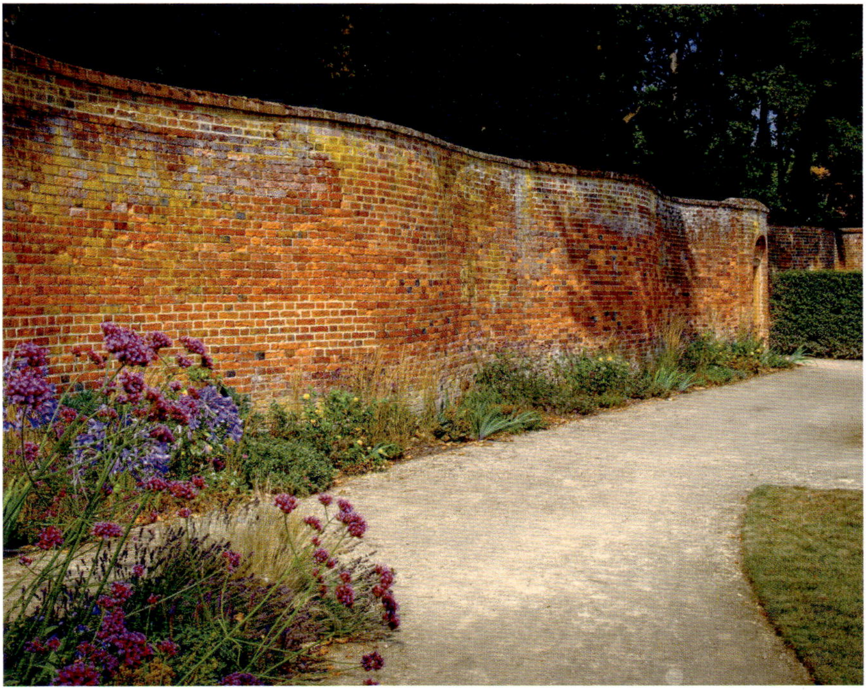

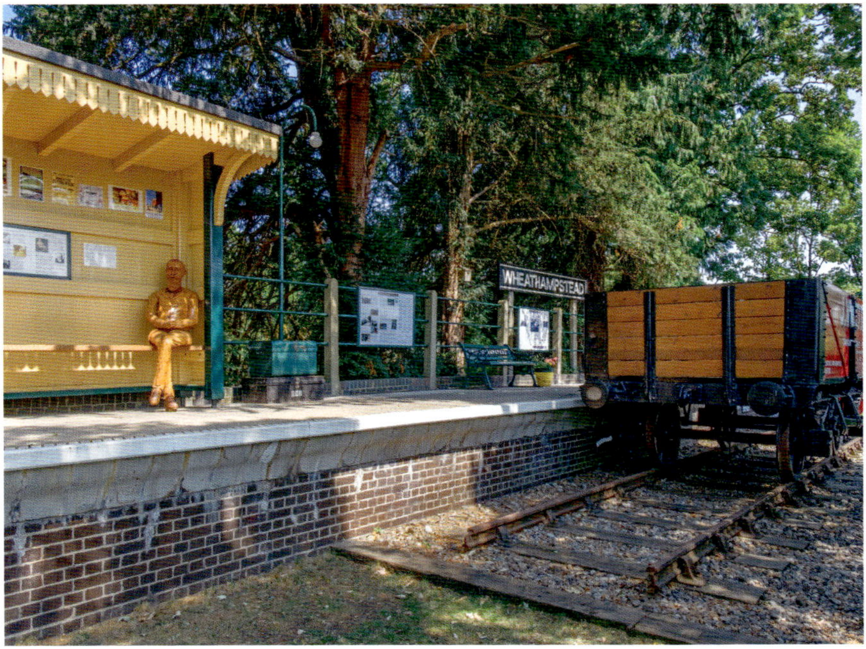
WHEATHAMPSTEAD

St. Leonard's Church
Flamstead

St. Leonard's Church is the focal point of the rural village of Flamstead. Construction of the church was started in the 1120s and it is now Grade I listed. Both the interior and exterior are considered exceptional because they have survived without substantial alteration since about 1450.

The church contains the most important medieval wall paintings in Hertfordshire outside St. Alban's Cathedral. Preserved for hundreds of years after being covered during the Reformation, they were rediscovered in the 1930s. Another delightful feature is a late medieval rood screen. A rare feature is a house built directly onto the church for the comfort of a 14th century priest.

In the churchyard, the 1811 tomb chest of Thomas Pickford, founder of the celebrated firm of carriers, is a Grade II listed monument in its own right.

Further Information

39

High Street, Flamstead, AL3 8BS.

www.churchfm.org
www.hertfordshirechurches.weebly.com/flamstead-church-hertfordshire

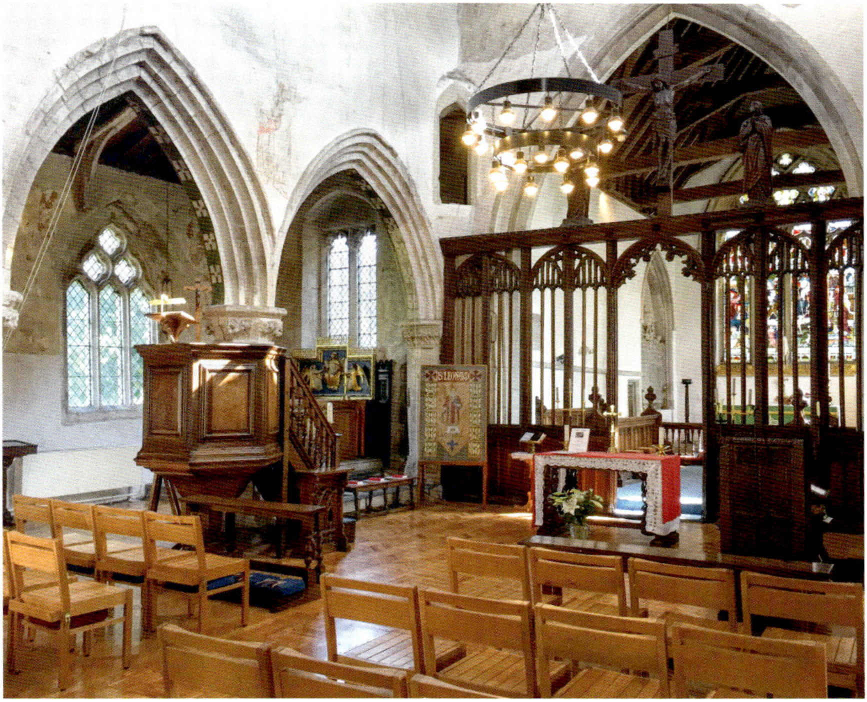

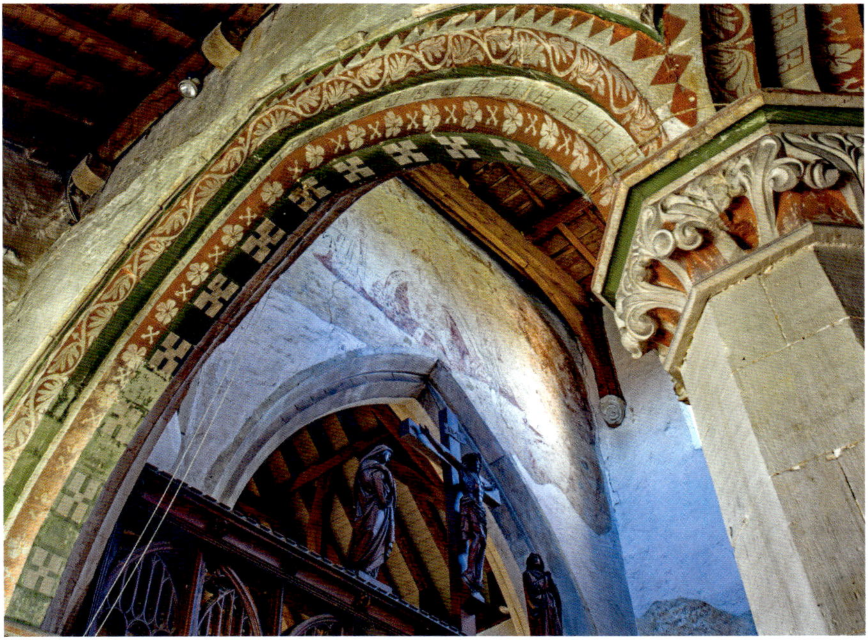

Ashridge Estate and the Bridgewater Monument
Berkhamsted

Ashridge Estate covers 5000 acres of the Chiltern Hills with ancient beech and oak woodlands, commons and chalk downs and is brimming with history. It ranges from the ancient hill fort at Ivinghoe Beacon to the magnificent park and woodland surrounding Ashridge House with past links to royalty, Capability Brown, the Duke of Bridgewater and both World Wars. The different landscapes support a variety of flora and fauna including carpets of bluebells, rare butterflies and fallow deer.

The Bridgewater Monument, built in 1832 as a memorial to the Duke who built the coal-carrying canal in North West England, towers over the estate. When open, a climb of the 172 steps affords views as far as London's Canary Wharf.

Further Information

40

Moneybury Hill, Ringshall, Berkhamsted, HP4 1LT.

www.nationaltrust.org.uk/ashridge-estate

Access: Advice is available from the visitor centre on the opening hours of the monument and on the many routes to explore on foot or by bike.

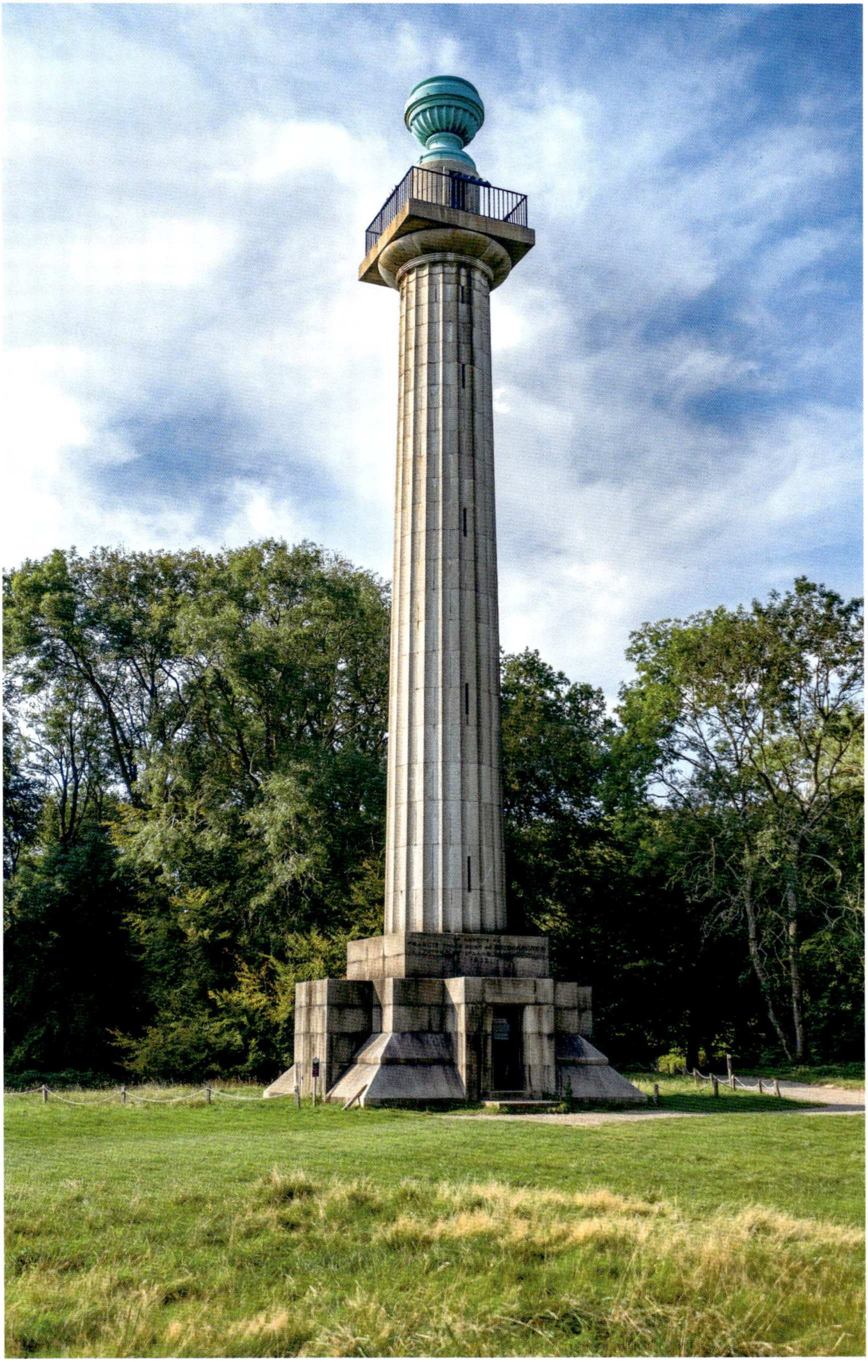

The Natural History Museum
Tring

Built in 1889, the Natural History Museum at Tring houses the incredible zoological collections of Lionel Walter Rothschild. His passion for the natural world resulted in one of the largest private natural history collections ever assembled. The building and collection were gifted to the nation in 1937 and became part of the Natural History Museum.

The museum retains its unique Victorian character, including its original floor-to-ceiling, glass-fronted, hardwood and iron cases. The 4,000 specimens displayed are still arranged in taxonomic order, classified into related groups, just as they were in Walter's lifetime. Highlights of the displays include extinct animals such as the Quagga and the Thylacine, one of the first emperor penguins to arrive in the UK, dressed fleas and a selection of the Natural History Museum's pedigree dog collection. Entrance is free but tickets must be booked in advance.

Further Information

41

The Walter Rothschild Building, Akeman Street, Tring, HP23 6AP.

www.nhm.ac.uk/visit/tring

Access: Entrance is free but tickets must be booked in advance.

Image: © The Trustees of The Natural History Museum, London

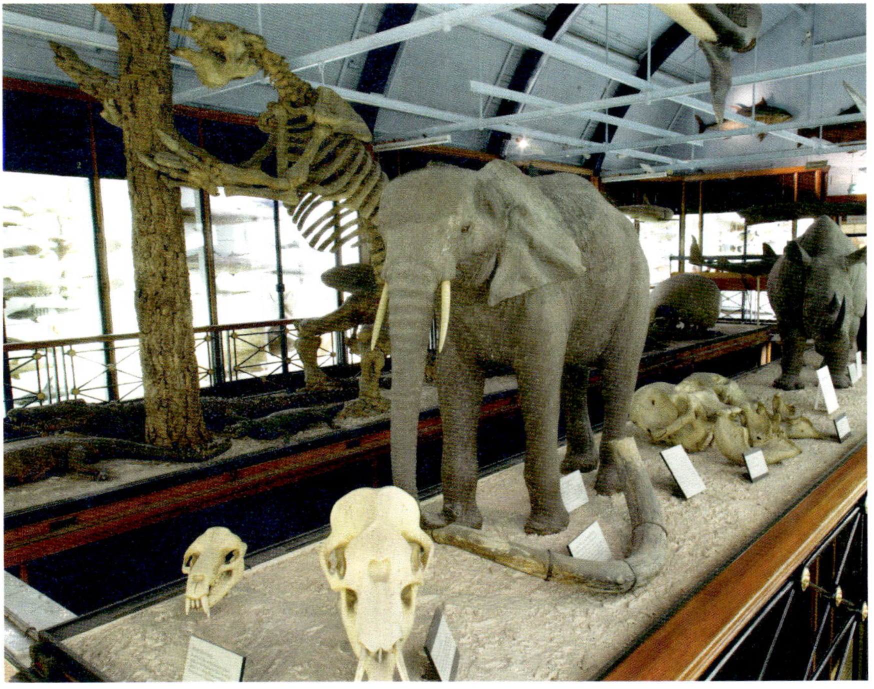

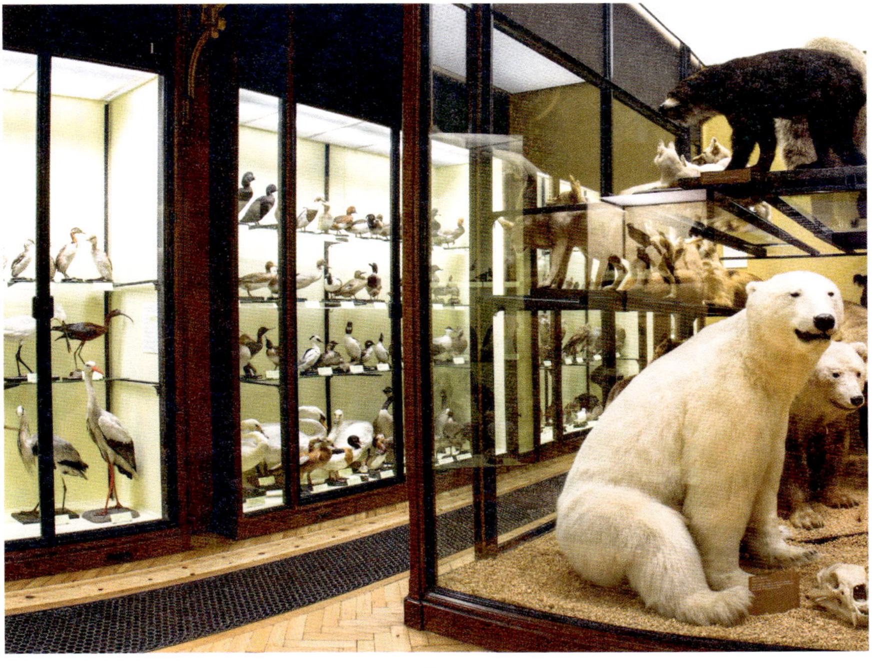

Berkhamsted Castle

Berkhamsted

This is one of England's oldest motte and bailey castles which is steeped in over 950 years of history, starting with William the Conqueror. The original timber castle was built because of Berkhamsted's strategic location on the route between London and the Midlands.

As Lord Chancellor, Thomas Becket began rebuilding the castle in stone and it became a favoured residence for royals over the centuries, from Edward III to the Black Prince, until it began falling into disrepair in the 16th century.

Entering the castle grounds reveals a peaceful, green space where it is possible to envisage the original motte and bailey. Remnants of the exterior walls, ditches and earthworks can be explored and a climb to the top of the motte will be rewarded with beautiful views of the surrounding area.

Further Information

42

White Hill, Berkhamsted, HP4 1LJ.

www.berkhamstedcastle.org.uk
www.english-heritage.org.uk/visit/places/berkhamsted-castle

Access: Open daily throughout the year. Free entry. Most terrain is suitable for buggies and wheelchairs. Guided tours can be arranged in advance.

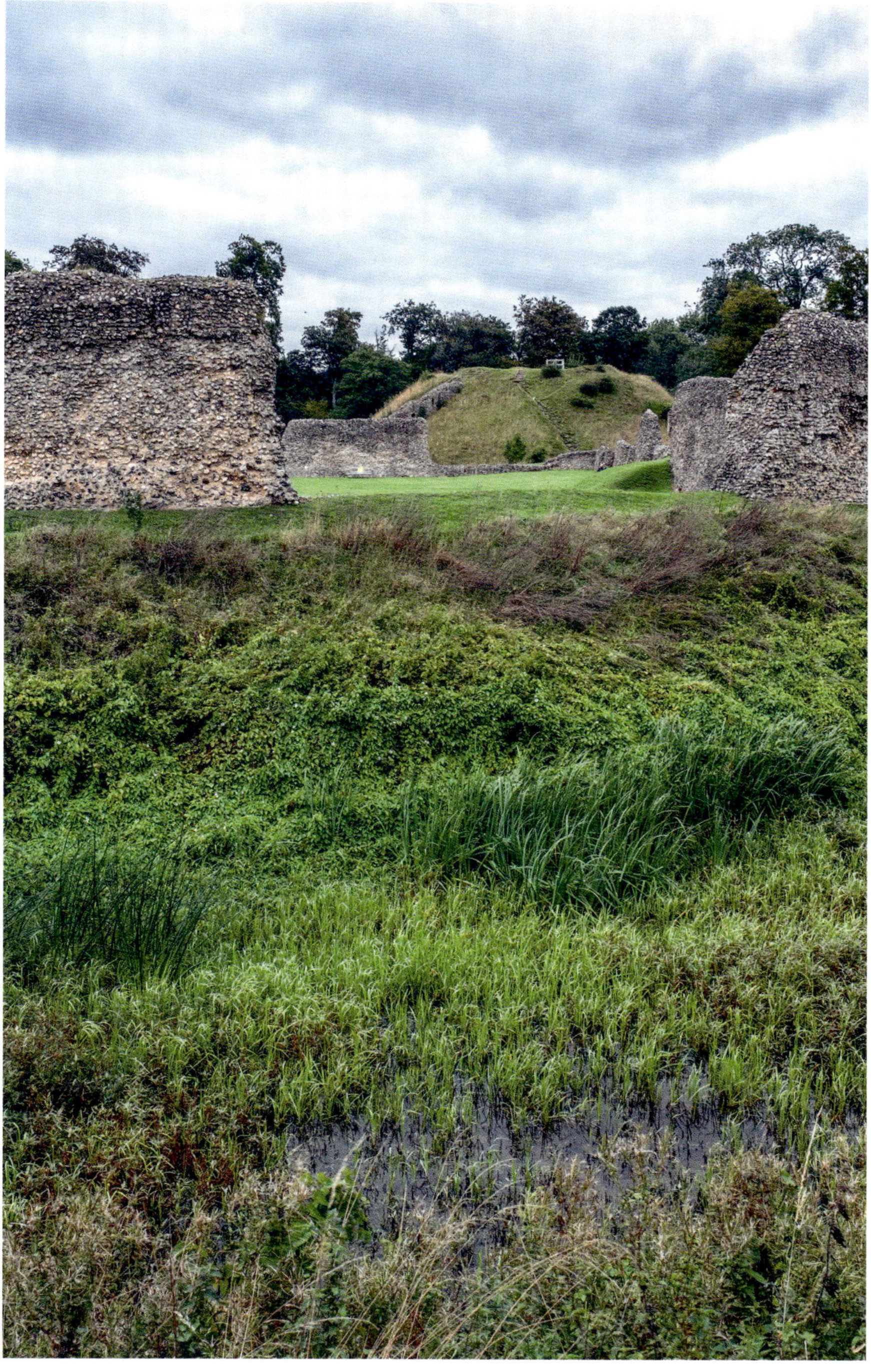

Piccotts End Wall Paintings
Hemel Hempstead

These wall paintings are a miraculous survival of early 16th century domestic decoration. Painted in the late 1520s, they would have been visible for only a few short years before the Reformation in England forced such "Popish" imagery to be destroyed.

The faces of Jesus and the Saints were carefully scratched away before the paintings were covered by a layer of coarse linen, subsequently overlaid with six different layers of wallpaper. They remained hidden until their accidental discovery by Arthur Lindley in 1953. Images depicted include Christ in Majesty; the Virgin Mary holding the body of Jesus; St. John wearing a camel skin during the baptism of Jesus; and St. Peter and St. Clement, unusually depicted in full Papal regalia.

These little-known paintings are extremely important as they provide an insight into the mindset of a member of the "middling" classes at this time of religious turmoil.

Further Information

43

132 Piccotts End, Hemel Hempstead, HP1 3AU.

www.piccottsendpaintings.uk

Access: Partakers in Heritage Open Days event. See website for details on how to book and for disabled access information. Free entry but small donation appreciated.

Image: © Courtesy of Karen Murphy.

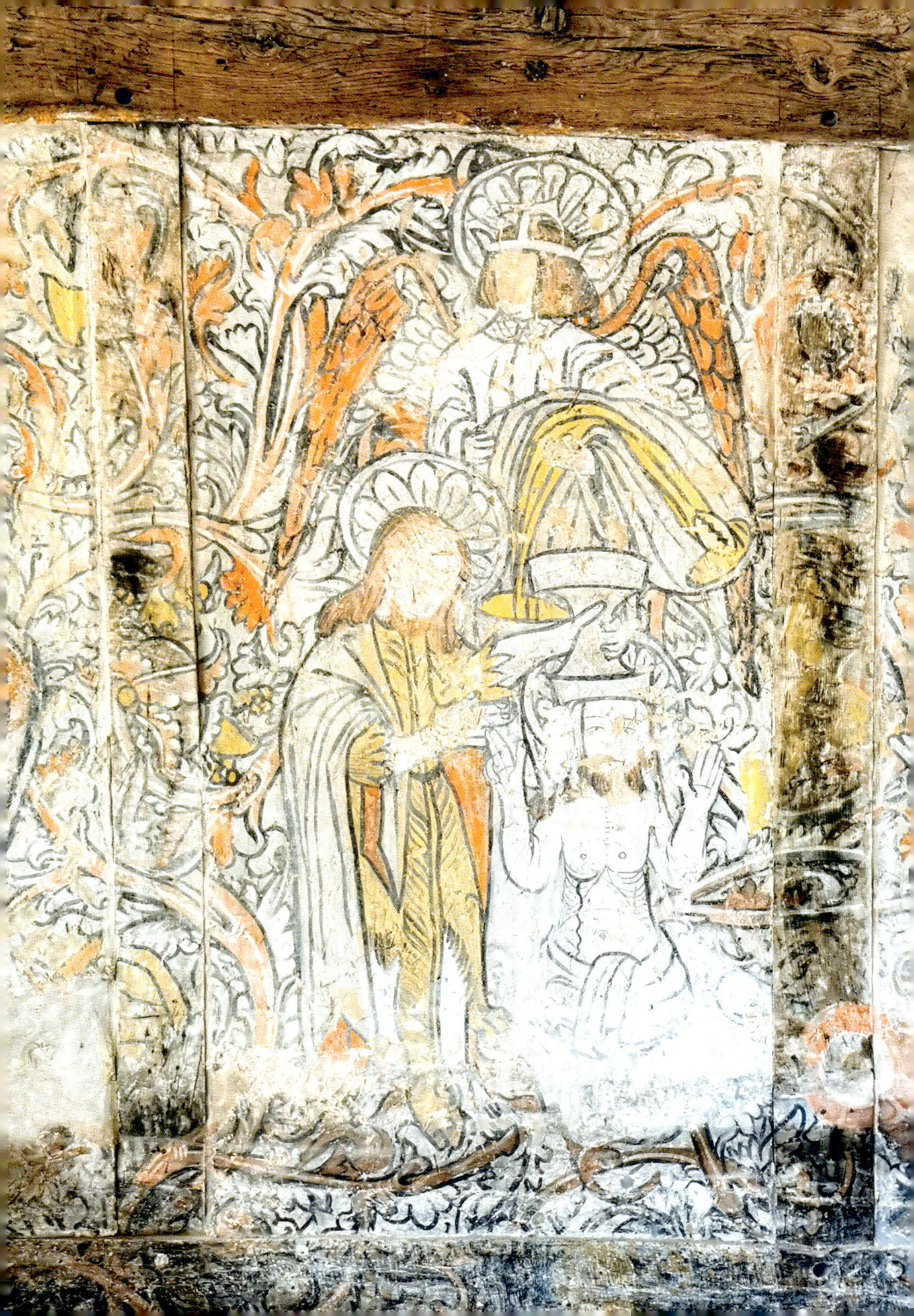

Frogmore Paper Mill
Apsley, Hemel Hempstead

In 1803, Frogmore Mill became the world's first mechanised paper mill, housing the newly patented Fourdrinier mechanical paper making machine. Owned for many years by The John Dickinson Stationery Company, the mill still operates one machine that is over 100 years old. There are displays of a wide range of equipment used throughout the ages, including fire engines.

Guided tours last 40-60 minutes, including learning about the 2000 year history of paper and the transition from handmade to machine made paper. Visitors have the chance to make their own sheet of paper to take home and often express wonder at seeing Fourdrinier machines in operation, still making paper using the same process used a century before.

Further Information

44

Fourdrinier Way, Apsley, Hemel Hempstead, HP3 9RY.

www.frogmorepapermill.org.uk

Access: Details of tours, opening hours for the shop, café, gallery and mill are on the website. Entry fees applicable.

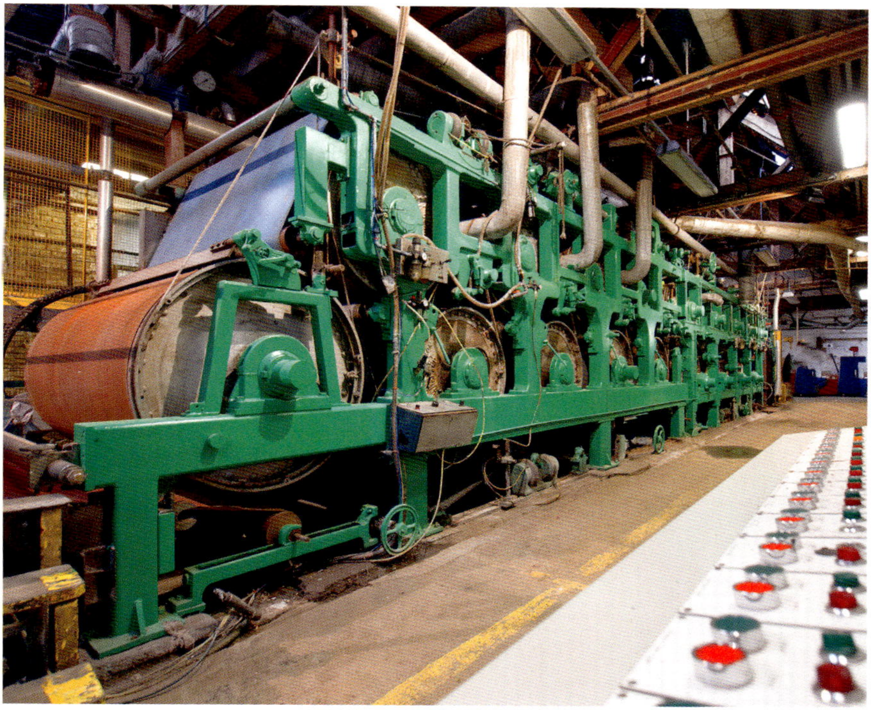

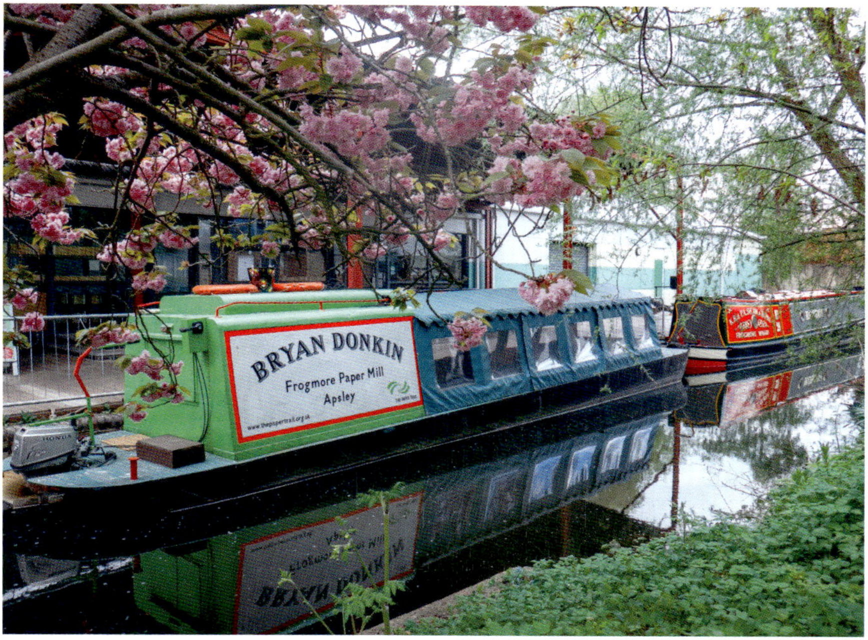
BRYAN DONKIN
Frogmore Paper Mill
Apsley

The Cathedral and Abbey Church of St. Alban

St. Albans

This magnificent building is steeped in history beginning in Roman times. It is the site of the original 4th century shrine to St. Alban, Britain's first Saint, and the foundation of a Benedictine Monastery in the 8th century. Henry V111 dissolved the Abbey in the 16th century and it became a cathedral in 1877.

The present structure, greatly renovated in Victorian times, is dominated by the Norman crossing tower which is believed to be the only existing cathedral tower in England built of Roman brick. The 85 metre nave, the longest in England, is notable for the beautifully preserved medieval wall paintings and features a stone screen originating in the 14th century and now remarkable for the colourful martyr statues added in 2015. A spectacular rose window is the highlight of the beautiful stained glass within the cathedral.

Further Information

45

Sumpter Yard, St. Albans, AL1 1BY.

www.stalbanscathedral.org

What's Nearby: Roman theatre ruins and city walls.
www.english-heritage-org.uk/visit/places/roman-wall-of-st-albans
www.gorhamburyestate.co.uk/The-Roman-Theatre

Image: © Courtesy of Luke Watson & St. Albans Cathedral.

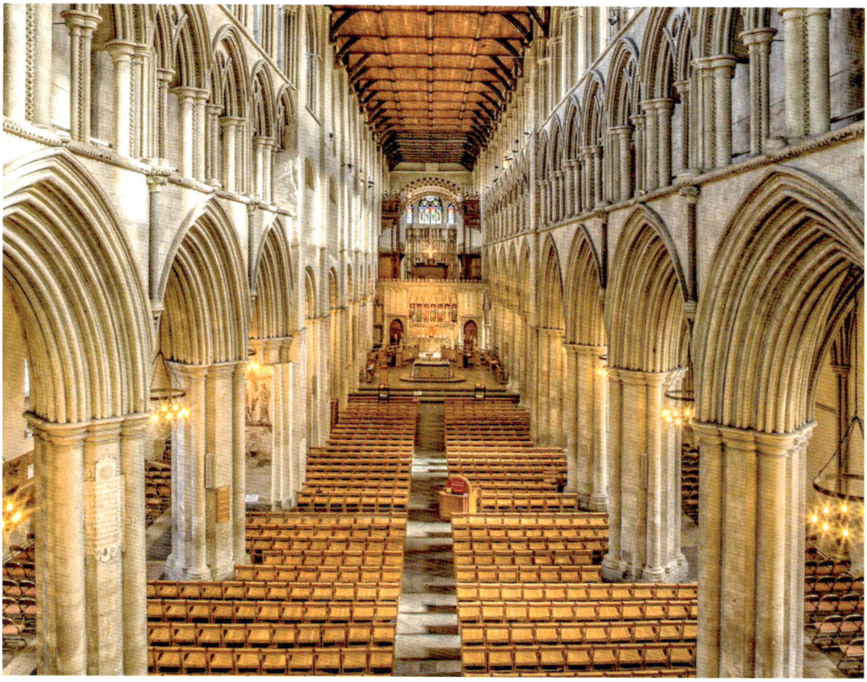

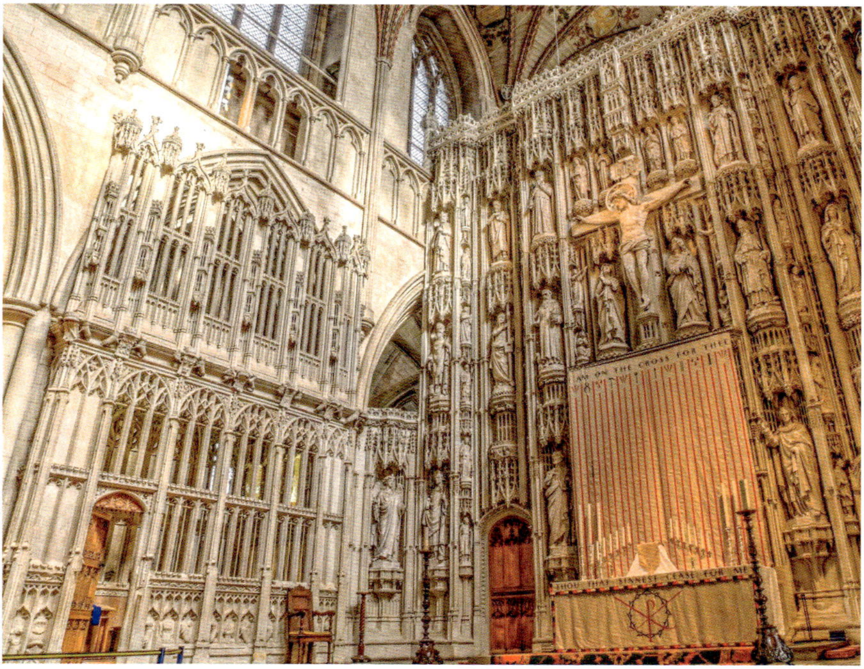
AM ON THE CROSS FOR THEE

St. Albans Museum and Gallery

The publishers of this book contributed funds for the development of this recently restored Georgian treasure which shows 2000 years of local and national heritage. In addition to a permanent exhibition, *The City that went Uphill*, charting the area's development from a pre-Roman settlement to the present day, there are regularly-changing art exhibitions.

The Georgian architecture of the splendid Assembly Rooms has been restored to the former glory of a venue originally used for balls, galas and concerts. The restoration of the historic Courtroom with its subterranean cells reveals the dramatic stories of law and order within the district. Visitors can also enjoy splendid rooftop views over the city.

Further Information

46

Town Hall, St. Peter's Street, St. Albans, AL1 3DH.

www.stalbansmuseums.org.uk/visit/st-albans-museum-gallery

Access: Open 7 days with free admission.

What's Nearby: Verulamium Museum.
www.stalbansmuseums.org.uk/visit/verulamium-museum
Climb the Clock Tower, the only surviving medieval town belfry in England.
www.stalbansmuseums.org.uk/visit/clock-tower
Samuel Ryder's (of Ryder Cup fame) seed building.
www.stalbanshistory.org/social-history/victorian-st-albans/samuel-ryder

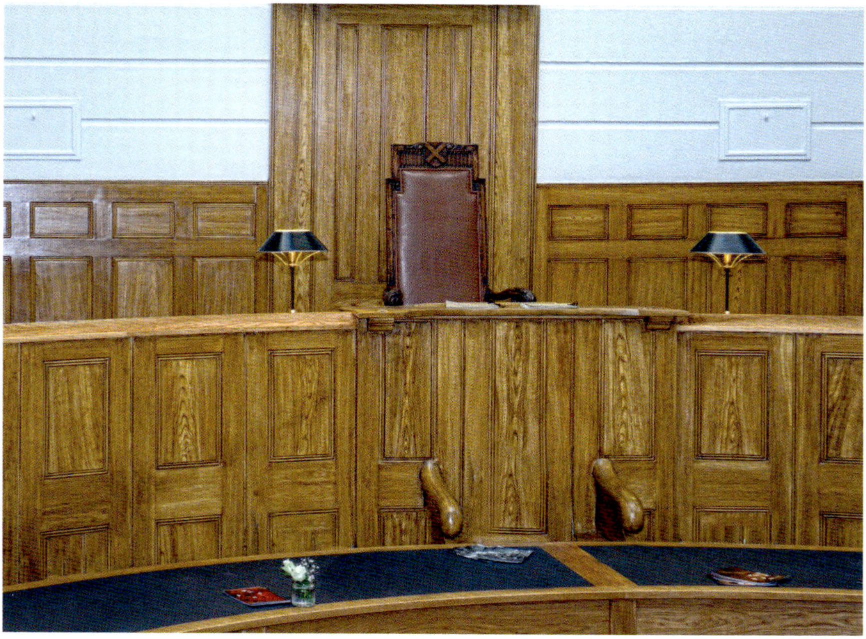

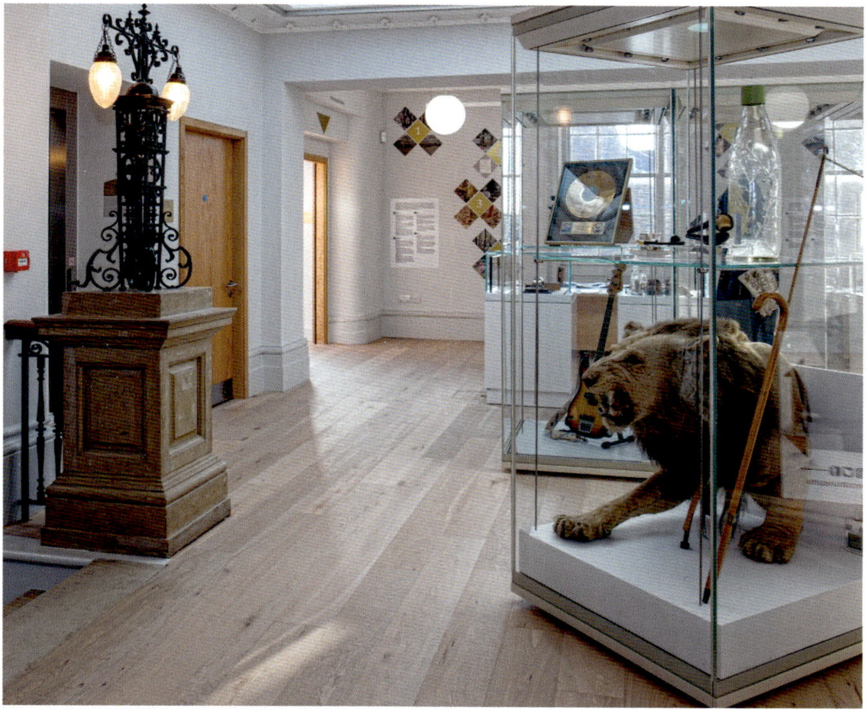

The de Havilland Aircraft Museum
London Colney

Located at the site of the historic Salisbury Hall in London Colney, the de Havilland Museum was the first aircraft museum in Britain when it opened to the public in 1959. The site is the subject of many historical references dating back to Roman times and the Domesday Book.

Many illustrious people have been associated with Salisbury Hall, ranging from 'Warwick the Kingmaker' and Nell Gwynne, Lady Randolph Churchill and the Young Winston, to Sir Nigel Gresley, designer of the Flying Scotsman and the Mallard. Aviation arrived here when, in 1939, the de Havilland Mosquito design team moved in as a security precaution. The Mosquito prototype and two other aircraft were assembled and flown from the surrounding fields before production was agreed and moved to other facilities.

The area is synonymous with de Havilland as its major factory was located at Hatfield.

Further Information

47

Salisbury Hall, London Colney, St. Albans, AL2 1BU.

www.dehavillandmuseum.co.uk

Access: Variety of guided tours, simulators and experiences available for various donations. Please check website for full details.

Image: © Courtesy of Lee Mullins.

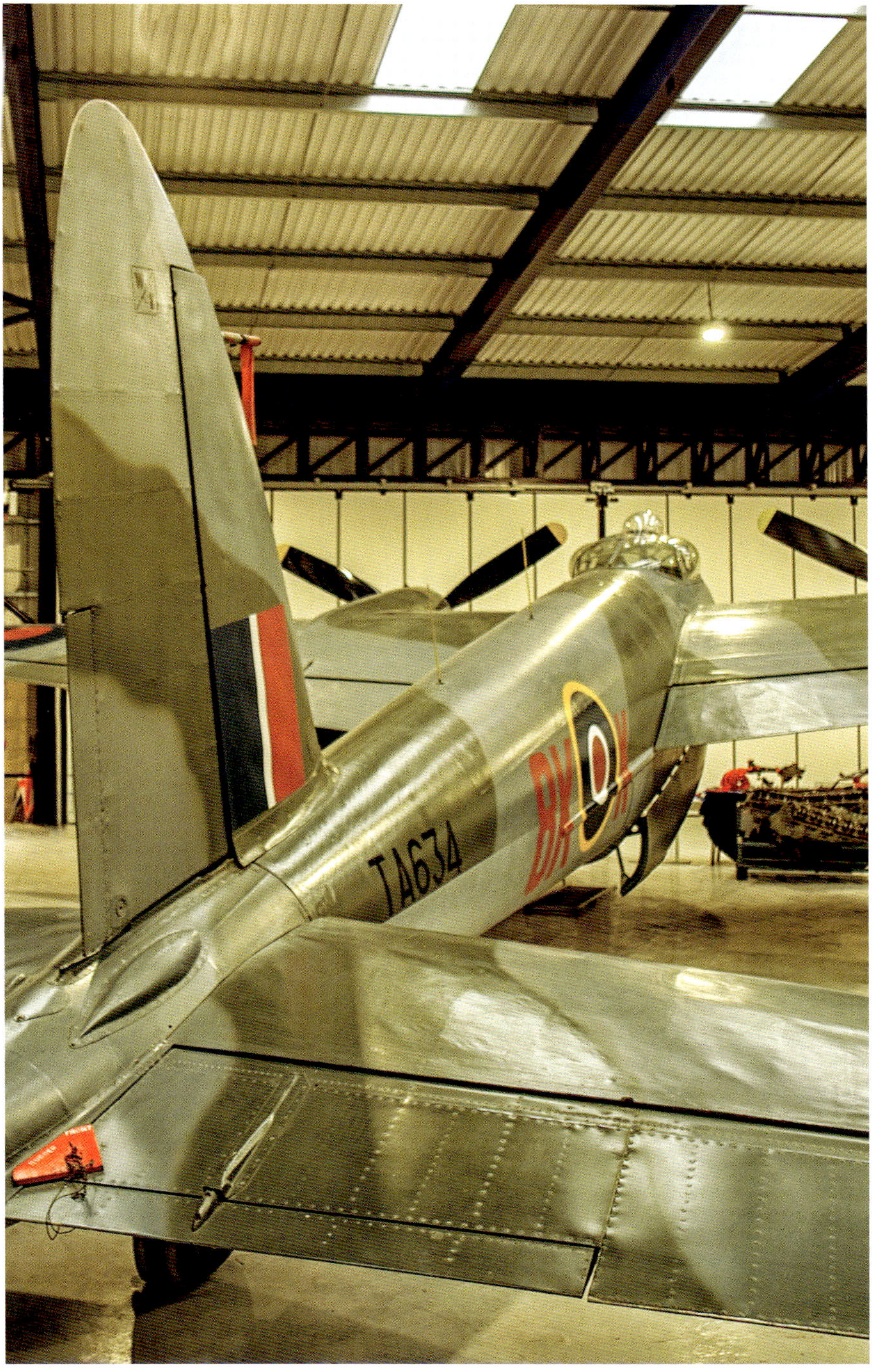
TA634

Jain Temple and Oshwal Centre

Potters Bar

The serenity and peaceful atmosphere of this hidden gem belies its location within sight of the M25. Set in 70 acres of countryside with manicured gardens, quiet walks and interesting sculptures, this was the first Jain temple to be built in Europe according to ancient Hindu design principles.

Consecrated in 2005, it is laid out in the Jain symbol for the Cosmos. The red stone exterior with its intricate carving and craftsmanship is in great contrast to the ornate marble interior. Guided tours are available by arrangement to explain the Jain religion. Mahatma Ghandi adopted the main tenets of the philosophy and non-violent way of living of this religion which originated in India in the 6th century BC.

Further Information

48

Coopers Lane Road, Northaw, Potters Bar, EN6 4DG.

www.oshwal.org.uk/oshwal-centre

What's Nearby: Fir and Pond Woods, this ancient woodland with medieval fish ponds and rare insect and bird life is situated opposite the Temple site.
www.hertswildlifetrust.org.uk/firandpondwoods

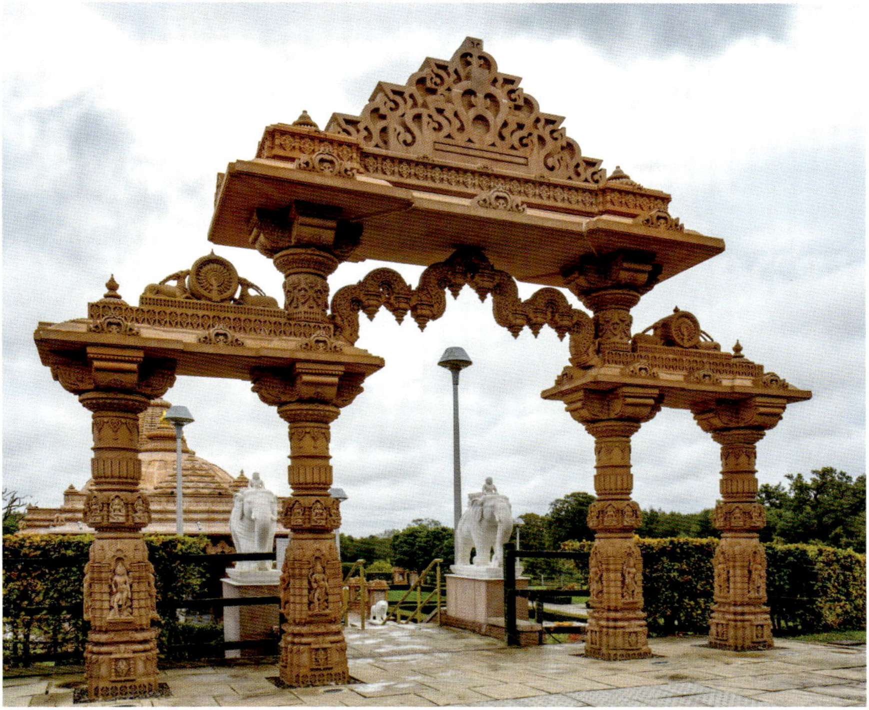

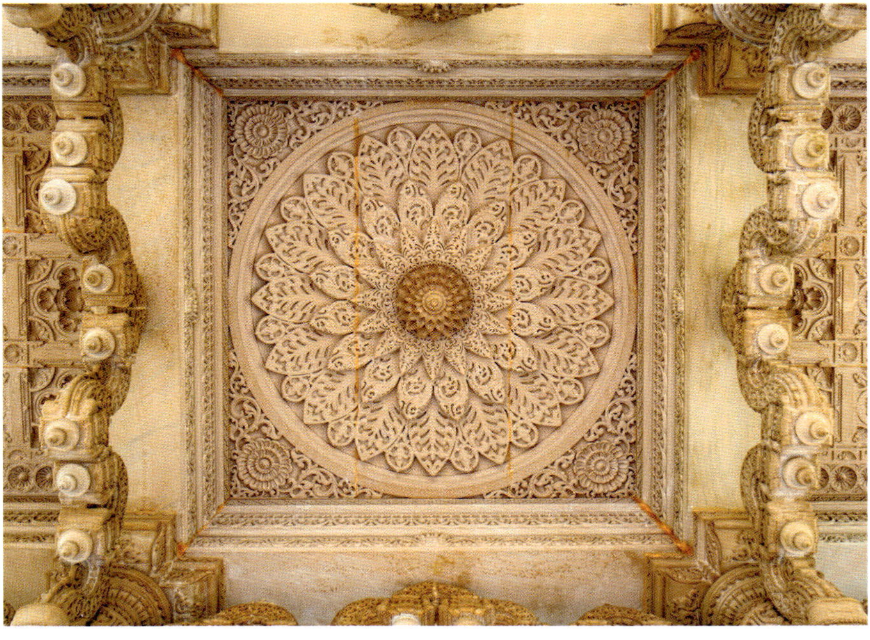

Bushey Museum & Art Gallery

The Bushey Museum & Art Gallery covers local history from early times with displays of archaeology, artefacts, documents and historical maps which illustrate Bushey's social and business heritage. The museum also represents Bushey's important artistic history with its collection of artwork of national significance. This includes paintings and drawings by the Monro Circle of artists, as well as items and ephemera relating to Sir Hubert von Herkomer's famous Art School in Bushey. There is also a major collection of paintings by Herkomer's student Lucy Kemp-Welch, most famous for her illustrations of Anna Sewell's 'Black Beauty', published in 1915.

Located in an Edwardian former council building, close to Bushey High Street, the museum offers a wealth of unexpected revelations and little-known facts concerning the unique history of this area.

Further Information

49

Rudolph Road, Bushey, WD23 3HW.

www.busheymuseum.org

Access: Free parking nearby with good wheelchair accessibility throughout - full details listed on website.

Image: *Our Village Nurse* by Sir Hubert von Herkomer R.A. (1849-1914).

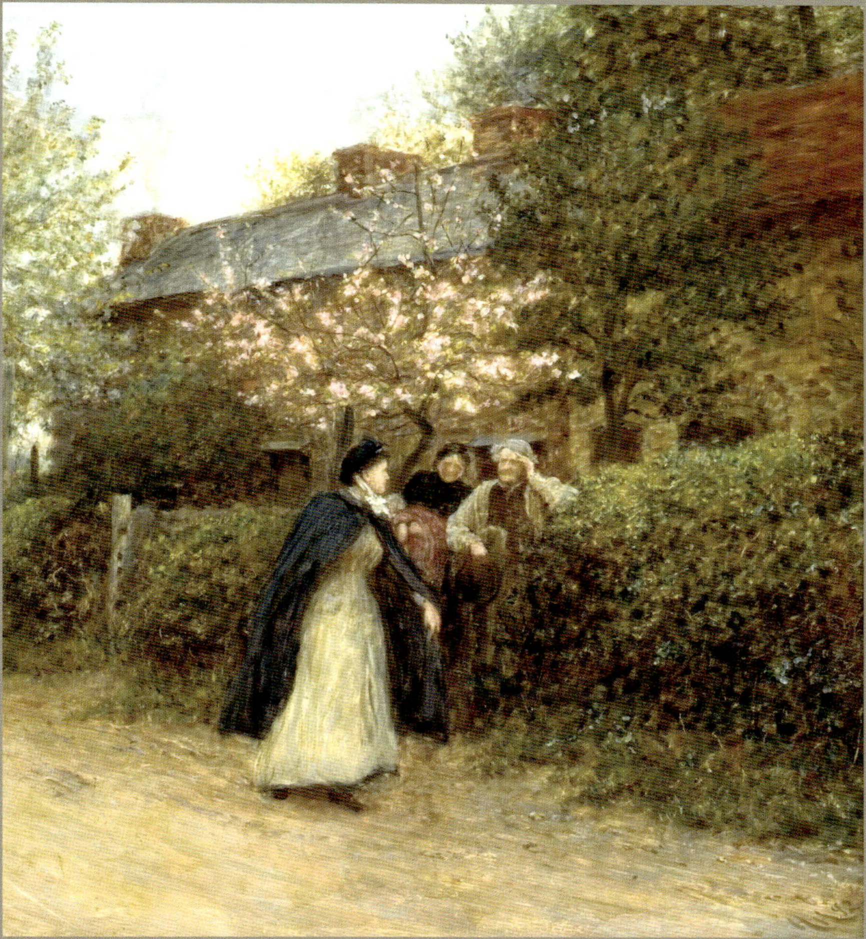

Moor Park Mansion

Rickmansworth

This Grade 1 listed building dating from the 1720s abounds with artistic and historic interest. The original 17th century mansion was embellished in the Palladian style by Sir James Thornhill. Sitting in over 300 acres of parkland, it is now a golf clubhouse.

Guided tours reveal the stories of residents, including Admiral Lord Anson, founder of the modern Navy and commissioner of landscaper Capability Brown, and the Grosvenors who introduced golf to Moor Park. During WW2 the mansion served as the headquarters of the 1st Airborne Corps where Operation Market Garden and the Battle of Arnhem were planned.

The interior's stunning features include paintings by Amigoni and an Antonio Verrio ceiling, as well as work by Robert Adam and a painted ceiling by Giovanni Batista Cipriani. A trompe l'oeil domed ceiling was reputedly inspired by St. Peter's in Rome.

Further Information

50

Moor Park Golf Club, Rickmansworth, WD3 1QL.

www.moorparkdfas.com/heritage-volunteers

Access: Advance booking required for monthly tours. Admission fee. Entrance ramp enables access for wheelchair users and there is a small lift.

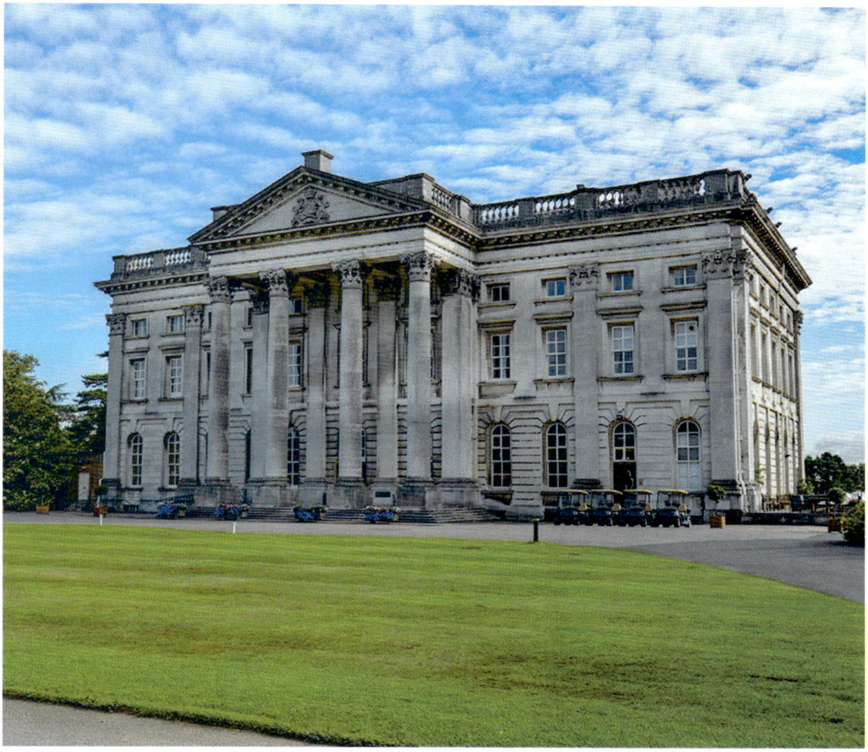

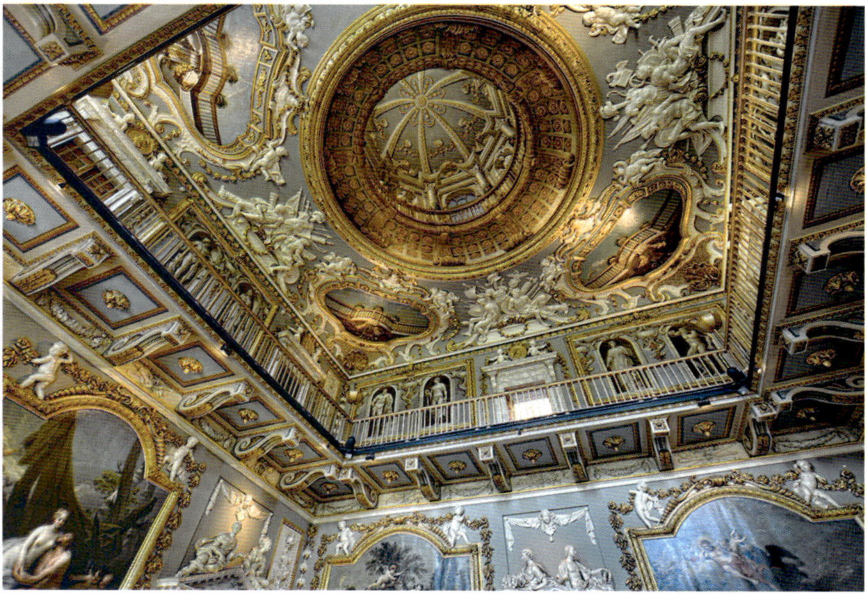

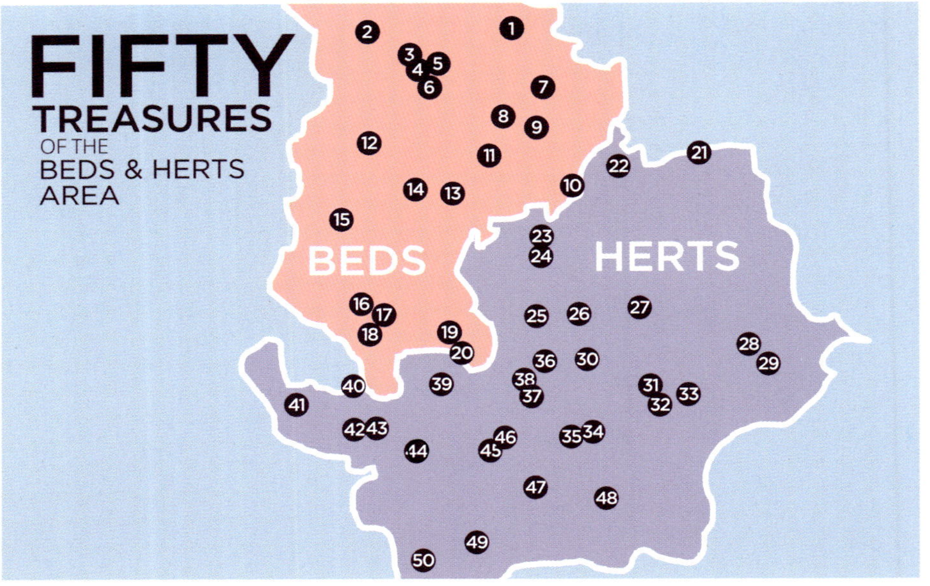

1 Congregational Chapel
2 Kathy Brown's Garden
3 Foster Hill Road Cemetery
4 Higgins Museum
5 Bunyan Meeting House
6 Elstow Village
7 The Lodge RSPB
8 Shuttleworth Collection
9 Jordans Mill
10 Stotfold Water Mill
11 Chicksands Priory
12 St. Mary the Virgin
13 Wrest Park
14 De Grey Mausoleum
15 Woburn Abbey
16 Totternhoe Knolls
17 Priory Church of St. Peter
18 Tree Cathedral
19 Stockwood Discovery Centre
20 Luton Hoo Estate Walled Garden
21 Royston Cave
22 St. Mary's Church
23 Lavender Fields
24 British Schools Museum
25 St. Paul's Walden Bury
26 Knebworth House
27 Benington Lordship
28 Forge Museum
29 Henry Moore Studios
30 Roman Baths
31 St. Michael & All Angels
32 Friends Meeting House
33 Scott's Grotto
34 Mill Green Museum
35 Hatfield House
36 Shaw's Corner
37 St. Helen's Church
38 Wheathampstead Village
39 St. Leonard's Church
40 Ashridge Estate
41 Natural History Museum
42 Berkhamsted Castle
43 Piccotts End Wall Paintings
44 Frogmore Paper Mill
45 St. Albans Cathedral
46 St. Albans Museum & Gallery
47 de Havilland Museum
48 Jain Temple & Oshwal Centre
49 Bushey Museum & Art Gallery
50 Moor Park Mansion

THE ARTS
SOCIETY
BEDS & HERTS

BEDS & HERTS AREA SOCIETIES

Ashridge DFAS	ashridgedfas.org.uk
Bishops Stortford DFAS	tasbs.org.uk
Bushey DFAS	busheydfas.org.uk
Chorleywood	chorleywoodfinearts.org
East Herts	theartssociety.org/east-herts
Gade Valley	theartssocietygadev.org.uk
Great Ouse Valley	theartssociety.org/great-ouse-valley
Harpenden Area	theartssocietyharpendenareadfas.org.uk
Harpenden Evening	tashe.org.uk
Moor Park	moorparkdfas.com
North Bedfordshire	theartssociety.org/north-bedfordshire
North Hertfordshire	theartssocietynorthherts.org.uk
Rickmansworth	tasrickmansworth.org.uk
St Albans	theartssociety.org/st-albans
Tring Park	artssociety-tringpark.co.uk
Welwyn Garden	theartssociety.org/welwyn-garden
Woburn	theartssociety.org/woburn-area

385
SOCIETIES

90,000
MEMBERS

12,000
VOLUNTEERS

362
LECTURERS

10
COUNTRIES

1
THE ARTS
SOCIETY

LECTURES

SPECIAL INTEREST DAYS

VISITS

TOURS

EVENTS

VOLUNTEERING PROJECTS

YOUNG ARTS

HERITAGE

ARTS FOR ALL

CONTACT

Find your nearest Society

www.theartssociety.org

The Arts Society is the operating name of the National Association of Decorative and Fine Arts Societies:
Registered Charity No. (England and Wales) 1089743
Registered Charity No. (Scotland) SC039240
Registered Company No. (England) 04307984